SOME PROBLEMS

OF

SOCIAL REFORM

IN

HINDU SOCIETY.

BY

LALA BAIJNATH, B·A.

OF THE

N.-W. P. Judicial Service.

AUTHOR OF

SOCIAL REFORM
IN THE N.-W. P., FIRST
IMPRESSIONS OF AN EDUCATED
HINDU OF ENGLAND AND PARTS OF
EUROPE (IN THE PRESS), LEGAL MAXIMS
IN URDU, EXPLAINED AND ILLUSTRATED WITH
REFERENCE TO THE LAWS OF BRITISH INDIA &c. &c.

———

ALIGARH.

PRINTED AT THE "INSTITUTE PRESS".

1891.

CONTENTS.

—+o+—

PREFACE ... ... I—VI

INTRODUCTION ... ... 1—3

POSITION OF WOMAN ... ... 3-—13

EARLY MARRIAGES ... ... 13—50

THE HINDU WIDOW ... ... 50 — 63

OTHER QUESTIONS OF SOCIAL REFORM.—

    SEA VOYAGES ... ... 63—69

    EXTRAVAGANCE IN MARRIAGE
    AND OTHER CEREMONIES } ... 69—71

    SHRADDHAS ... 71—73

    PILGRIMAGES ... ... 73—74

    GENERAL CHARACTERISTICS OF
    MODERN HINDU SOCIETY } ... 74—76

CONCLUSION ... ... 76—80

NOTE.—I regret that mistakes have crept in printing and request the reader to correct them according to the following :—

CORRIGENDA.

—o—

Page	line	for	read
3	8	qeustion	question
4	Note line 1	Arauyaha	Aranyaka
5	24	put him	put to him
8	13	than i e	than
„	14	the making	making
„	15	is, now	is now,
9	28	portaion	portion
14	7	are evil	are an evil
22	15	those those	those
27	27	writer	writers
Note 27	...	Montegazza	Mantegazza
Note 32	35	easte	caste
34	17	shakal	jackal
39	17	miscondct	misconduct
40	25	Panal	Penal
45	Note 30	the Inspector	an Inspector
52	13	ofter	after
54	1	Sadhia	Sadhivi
56	27	anxions	anxious
61	14	welll	well
62	23	the assist	to assist
„	28	so all	to all
67	24	premanently	permanently
68	5	word	a word
„	11	perfers	prefers
69	29	$\frac{2}{3}$rds	of $\frac{2}{3}$rds
71	18	Brirish	British

PREFACE.

This is a revised and greatly enlarged edition of the second portion of my pamphlet on Social Reform in the North-Western Provinces, published in 1886, a second edition of the portion relating to Mr. Malabari's tour in those Provinces, having already been published by him in Bombay at the end of the last year. The papers on early marriages as well as on the position of the Hindu widow, have been entirely re-written with reference to the new light that has since been thrown on the subject, and several new papers on other subjects of social reform, for instance female education, the increase of population, the much debated Age of Consent Bill, the curtailment of marriage and other expenses, the disabilities attending sea voyages, &c. have been added with a view to direct public attention to these important questions relating to the well-being of the Hindu society. Since the first edition of the book was published, I have had the advantage of a short visit to England, and the result of what I learnt in that country, as well as in other parts of Europe, has been partly embodied in these notes. The question of social reform has now passed beyond the stage of speculative discussion. On the contrary no Indian question has evoked a more sympathetic response in England than this question of raising the position of the women of India, and the committee that has been formed in that country is the most influential committee ever formed there for the agitation of any Indian question for some time. In India also, with the exception of that party of reactionists who wilfully shut their eyes to proved facts, the necessity of social reform is largely admitted. Only differences of opinion prevail among the educated section of the community upon the methods of operation, and while a very large class of thinkers say that it is not the business of the Government but of the people, to carry out the work of social reform, another equally large class advocates Government interference. My own view of the question will be found in a paper specially devoted to this subject in the body of the notes. I may however say that trusting to time and providence and leaving these important questions to take care of themselves, are not synonymous with deprecating Government interference. On the contrary while the Government may be left or even asked to interfere in matters which are opposed to humanity or public policy, the reformers cannot be relieved of their task of directing their own private efforts towards the removal of practices or customs which are beyond the province of the Legislature. What those practices are, I have tried to explain in the body of the notes, and I have no doubt that the present impetus given to the cause of social reform will result in more active private effort being brought about towards their removal. I have taken care not to preach what could not be put to practice either in the case of individuals or communities, only some courage of conviction like that shown by those who have been successful in carrying out social reform is required.

The question is frequently asked what is the Hindu *Shastra*. Says Krishna in the Bhagwad Gita,—"He who disregarding the ordinances of the *Shastra* follows his own inclination, does not attain perfection, nor happiness, nor the highest bliss. Therefore let *Shastra* be thy authority in determining what should or should not be done." (Chap. 16. 23. 24). There are however great differences of opinion as to what is binding as Shastra. Is it the *Vedas*, or the *Smritis*, the *Sutras*, or the *Puranas* or the *Ithihasas*, or all these, or is it the dogmas of modern text writers or those of the founders of the various schools of philosophy or sects of religion? My answer is that the Hindu Shastra is *pre-eminently* the *Vedas*, and that all the other Shastras are only binding so far as they are in accordance with those ancient sources of the Hindu religion. The Vedas which are four in number, the Rig, Yajur, Sama and Atharva, are each divided into (1) the Samhita or the Mantra portion which contains the prayers, (2) the Brahmanas which contain rules for the application of the *Mantras* and (3) the *Upanishads* which contain the philosophy of religion. All these are of binding authority. After the Vedas come the *Sutras*, which also consist of three portions, the *Grihya*, the *Srauta* and the *Brahma* Sutras. The first treat of the various ceremonies to be performed on various occasions of life, the second give the rules of sacrifice by a rich householder, and the third deal with the philosophy of religion, and these are binding after the Vedas. The institutes of Manu, Yagya valkaya, Goutama, Parasara and other writers come next and among these Manu, Yagyavalkaya and Goutama are considered to be the principal authorities. Some of these Smritis, no doubt, contain contradictions. But they are more apparent than real and are often reconcileable. The great Epics, the Mahabharata and the Ramayana, the eighteen Maha Puranas and the eighteen minor Puranas, are the next binding authorities and wherever they contain contradictions, they are only to be followed in so far as their teachings are not inconsistent with those of the Vedas or the principal Smritis. The works of text writers like the author of the Mitakshara, or those of founders of schools of philosophy like Shankaracharya and Ramanuja, come under the same rule and the question in all cases should be whether a particular doctrine that is cited in support of or in opposition to any modern practice, is found in the ancient sources of the Hindu religion or is a merely accretionary dogma of later writres, added to ancient texts from local exigencies. As has been so forcibly pointed out by His Excellency the Viceroy in his speech on the Age of Consent Bill, there is no religion more encumbered by superimposed traditions, and more hampered by accretions of doubtful value than the Hindu religion. Therefore while it is necessary for the Government of this country to be cautious that religion is not allowed to block the way of reforms demanded in the interests of humanity and that where there is a conflict between religion and morality, the Government is bound to distinguish between essentials and non-essentials, between the fundamental principles of the religion concerned and the subsidiary beliefs and the accretionary dogmas which have accidentally grown up round them, it is more the duty of the

Hindus to assist the Government by pointing out what agrees with their true religion and what does not. For instance the practices of infant marriages, the enforced celibacy of Hindu widows, the prohibition of sea voyages and many other customs of Hindu society so frequently criticized are not at all sanctioned by its true religion but by later accretionary dogmas, and nothing has been more painful than the spectacle of Hindus taking their stand upon these dogmas for the defence of customs which have been proved to be not only opposed to their ancient and purer religion but repugnant to all ideas of humanity.

Since the notes were in type the Age of Consent Bill has been passed into law, and with the assurances given by His Excellency the Viceroy, of the Government closely watching the operation of the new law, and of its being prepared to provide additional safeguards if those given at present prove insufficient, I think there should be now no apprehension of harrassing prosecutions following the measure. The Hindu public cannot be too grateful for His Excellency for the statesmanlike tone in which he has replied to objections which from their very nature were mostly unfounded, and I think that that (community will be wise in taking his suggestion in so reforming their marriage customs and in making their girls not visit their husbands before the age of 12, as to render prosecutions under the Act to be unnecessary. They should also take the hint that has been thrown to them in moving the Government to invalidate marriages below the age of 12 and thus render the operation of the new law still further unnecessary. The Government does not seem to be at all unwilling to move in this respect and I hope the people will not fail to move it in the proper manner.

Of the great value of Mr. Malabari's efforts, of his devotion to this cause, and of his immense self-sacrifice, I have already spoken in my preface to the other portion of this book. Here I would only say that unless the Hindus themselves have many more men of Mr. Malabari's stamp not in one place or province, but in every town and province of India, the question of social reform shall not be fully solved. The sphere of the Legislature is after all a very limited sphere, while private individual and co-operative effort can always do much more in these matters and it is time that our people should learn to discriminate between the two.

It now remains for me to acknowledge the great help I have derived from my friend Mr. Dyaram Giddumal's excellent collection of opinions on the Position of Woman in India as well as from that learned book by Mr. R. C. Datt—the History of Civilization in Ancient India. My sincerest thanks are also due to Mr. T. W. Arnold, Professor of Philosophy in the M. A.-O. College, Aligarh, for kindly going over the proofs when the work was passing through the press as well as for making many valuable suggestions likely to increase its usefulness.

Aligarh,

March, 1891. }

BAIJNATH.

SOME PROBLEMS

OF

SOCIAL REFORM

IN

HINDU SOCIETY.

INTRODUCTION.

The study of the growth of the present social institutions of Hindu society is, at this moment when such a large amount of public attention is being directed to it, of peculiar importance, for while that society is admittedly largely in need of reform, the danger on the one hand is, of such reform taking a direction which may not be in accordance with its religious institutions or on the other hand of its being postponed indefinitely under the mistaken belief that the institutions of that society are perfect or that it would be a dangerous interference with its religion to meddle with them. The country is passing through that stage of transition which the contact of two civilizations necessarily brings about and while the reformers appeal to their ancient scriptures as paramount authorities on all subjects of reform, those who are opposed to them also appeal to the same source in support of their doctrines, and the question may well be asked whether the Hindu scriptures support the case of both the contending parties or only of one of them. It may also be questioned by an outside public whether this appeal to the scriptures is justified under the altered conditions of Hindu society, and whether practices which have now no reason to support them should be adhered to, merely because they happen to find support from texts which have lost all their force. And it is with the object of showing how far scriptural texts support or are opposed to some of the more objectionable customs of Hindu society, how far such customs are opposed to reason and common sense and what injury they have done to that society, that the present papers are written.

The ancient laws as well as the ancient customs of the Aryan race never sanctioned the present seclusion of women, nor enjoined their being kept in the state of ignorance in which they are now kept, nor their being married so early as they are now married, nor the enormous expenditure now incurred on their marriages nor the present hard and fast prohibitions of inter-marriages between the same sections of a caste. The Shastras never prohibitted voyages to foreign countries nor did they sanction the present indulgence in drink or other articles of food so repugnant to the proverbially pure and frugal habits of the Hindu, nor that system of blackmailing which is now-a-days so common at places of pilgrimages in India. On the contrary without saying that the country was a veritable paradise in the past, it may, I think, be said without fear of contradiction that the habits of living inculcated by the Hindu sages and law-givers of old were habits eminently calculated to lead to that higher and spiritual life, which they so constantly enjoined as the highest and only object of man's birth and which so many of their followers even in these days of high-pressure civilization successfully attain. Such an inquiry as would stimulate the Hindus to emulate their sages of old more closely than they have hitherto done, as well as show to the outside public how a country, after having attained that pitch of spiritual perfection which India rightly claims to have done in the past, could have been reduced to its present condition, cannot but be of much general interest.

(1) POSITION OF WOMAN.

The first qeustion therefore that I shall take up is the position of woman in India; this being the best test of the civilization of a country. The Shastras furnish clear evidence of the fact that both in the Vedic as well as in the Smriti (the Institutes of Manu and other writers) and the Epic periods, the position of woman in India was much better and infinitely more honourable than it is at present. In the Rigveda for instance we read of wives joining their husbands at sacrifices as well as of ladies composing hymns and leading the lives of Rishis. Every reader of the Upanishads is also familiar with the well-known stories of Maitreyi the wife of Yagyavalkya learning *Gyana* (spiritual knowledge) from her husband and of Gargi putting him the most abstruse questions on the creation of the universe. Says Maitreyi to Yagyavalkya " My lord, if the whole of this earth full of wealth belonged to me, should I be immortal by it ? " " No," replied Yagyavalkya, " like the life of rich people will be thy life." She then asked him to tell her how she could be happy and Yagyavalkya after saying that she was truly dear to him proceeded to unfold to her the highest truths of the philosophy of the Upanishads, concluding by saying " The Self (atman) is to be described by " not this " "not this". He is incomprehensible for he cannot be comprehended, he is imperishable for he cannot perish. He is unattached for he does not attach himself, he is unfettered for he does not suffer, he does not fail. Thus far goes immortality."* In the same Upanishad Yagyavalkya is described as having defeated in argument all the Brahmans at the court of Janaka, when a lady named Gargi came forward to defeat him in argument. She put him two questions, one of which was.—"That of which they say that it is above the heavens, beneath the earth, embracing heaven and earth, past, present and future, tell me in what it is woven like warp and woof." "In the Akshara, the imperishable, the unseen but seeing, the unknown but the knowing," replied the Rishi and Gargi after having realized the truth of the answer told the irritated Brahmans that Yagyavalkya was unconquerable in argument.

The Institutes of Manu have also texts like the following :

" Women are to be honoured and adorned by fathers and brothers, by husbands, as also by brothers-in-law who desire much prosperity.

Where women are honoured, there the gods rejoice ; but where they grieve, that (family) never prospers.

Houses, which women, not honoured, curse, as if blighted by magic, perish utterly.

Therefore they are ever to be honoured at ceremonies and festivals, with ornaments, clothes, and food, by men who desire wealth." (Book. III-55,56, 57—59.)

---

* Brihad Arauyaba Upanishad Adhyaya
2. Brahman 4. verses 3. et seq.
Ibid Adhyaya III Brahman 8, verses 7. et seq.

In the Epics also the heroines Sita and Draupadi are described as possessed of much intelligence. In fact they reason with their husbands more as equals than as inferiors. The impassioned appeal of Sita insisting to accompany Rama in his exile, the eloquent speech of Draupadi urging Yudhisthara to bestir himself to recover his lost kingdom, the courage of Damayanti under misfortune when left alone in a jungle, and the indignant reply of Sakuntala when discarded by her husband who had denied his marriage with her, could not have come from women who were ignorant or kept under the seclusion in which women are now kept in Hindu society. In the dramatic period the case also appears to be the same as in the Vedic and the Smriti periods and the popular legend of the great poet Kalidasa having been selected as her husband by a royal princess whom he had defeated in argument, shows that women were taught not only reading and writing but that some of them could solve also the highest problems of Hindu philosophy. In those days music and singing were also considered as desirable female accomplishments in the higher classes, for we read in the Sakuntala of the past having been recalled to the mind of king Dushyanta by tunes which his queen had played before him. Even the founder of Buddhism admitted his wife to and founded an order of female devotees, saying, in reply to a question put him, that women were capable of entering the second path or that of *arhatship*. The precepts of Gautama Buddha only followed the Brahamanic lawgivers in enjoining husbands to treat their wives with respect and kindness, to be faithful to them, to make others honour them, and wives, besides the duties of faithfulness and obedience, to show their skill and usefulness in domestic matters.

How was then the present position of Indian females brought about, how was it that sentiments like those mentioned above could give place to ideas which associated all that was evil with the name of woman, which described her to be a snare or which enjoined her being kept under restraint and ignorance or her being given away in marriage at an early age or even in her infancy ? The answer lies in the degeneration of the Kshatriya and the Vaishya classes, in the neglect of the study of their religious books by the latter, in the increase of the power of the priestly class, in their monopolizing the right to study the ancient scriptures and in their interpolating in them or construing them as best suited their interest. An ignorant laity encouraged a dogmatic and mysteriously superstitious priesthood, which taking advantage of the ignorance as well as the religious tendencies of its disciples gave its most absurd and unreasonable dogmas the authority of religion. Otherwise absurdities like a girl being a Gauri at eight years of age, a Rohini at nine, a maiden at ten and menstruant after that, and her father, mother and elder brother going to hell in case she menstruated without being married, could not have found place in some of the later religious writings of the Hindus. The climax was reached when Mahomedan invaders spread themselves over India and began to commit violence on Hindu girls and did not in their own lives set any high ideal of morality for their subjects. Men among whom concubinage and polygamy were recognized by their religion, and whose license was only checked by their inability to gratify their desires, could not have set any noble examples to their subjects, and so complete was the destruction of the political life of the Hindus, so complete the ignorance of the outside world and, as a result of all this, so great the hold of the priestly classes on the rest of the community, that sayings which would now excite a smile of contempt or dogmas which have a sad lesson to teach, came to be implicitly believed in by all those who boasted of the sublime teachings of their Upanishads or who loved to recite the adventures of heroes whose lives were vastly different from what their modern teachers had taught them. There could have been no national unity or national life under a system which degraded all the arts and all the industries and which made the rest of the community the slaves of their priests. This is the only possible explanation of the origin of practices which have neither reason nor commonsense but only perverted teachings of religion to support them. At the same time so long has been the period of this mental darkness and so great the repressive influences at work in Hindu society in the past, that these unreasonable and absurd teachings have now acquired all the force of custom and the task of the seeker of reform in Hindu society is not only to appeal to the purer sources of the Hindu religion but also to knock at the superstitious respect the Hindus bear for these later unmeaning innovations. The fight now-a-days is against erroneous, prevailing beliefs and customs and the reformer who cites the texts of the Vedas or the Smritis has also to refute innovations supported by texts of later writers which have a greater hold upon the community. There is no other alternative for him but to fight the battle in both ways by appealing to scriptures which all Hindus profess to respect as well as by citing reason to his aid in showing the pernicious character of the present practices. This has been the line followed by all those who are working in the cause of reform and I have also adopted it in these notes.

The influence of education and the various other agencies that have of late been very actively at work in India have made the question of the position of woman one of practical politics and the latter has lately evoked a more sympathetic response outside India than any other Indian question, and the day is not far distant when the women of India shall have their proper position in Indian society. Before this is done no concession of political privileges will make the Hindus great as a nation, nor, unless the old Persian saying " *Himmat mardan madad Khuda*" " Heaven helps those who help themselves" is more largely reduced into practice than *i. e.* has hitherto been done by the making the training of their women other than what it is, now is there any hope of advancement for the Hindus in the scale of nations. Our women, even more than our priests, are the greatest stumbling blocks in the way of progress and, unless their education is largely improved, no improvement in the education of the male portion of the laity will bring about the desired result, and this naturally leads me to the first of the most important means of raising the position of women in India, viz. progress of female education.

What has hitherto been done in this direction is but a small and infinitesimal part of what remains to be done. The Government thinks

Female Education.

that unless the natives themselves co-operate with it more largely than they have hitherto done, as well as show less indifference than they have hitherto shown in the matter

of female education, no permanent or satisfactory progress
can be hoped for, and that before any system of
improved female education could be adopted the natives
of the country should show that they are prepared for it. But
while agreeing with much of what the Government says and
while fully deploring the want of active exertion shown by
the natives in not taking an active share in female education
as they have done in that of males, one may be tempted to
ask whether the Government have also shown the same
activity in this matter as they have done in the matter of male
education and whether they have themselves left the field to
be explored by missionaries whose zenana missions and female
schools have, in spite of their proselyting character, done much
good work in this direction. The matter was fully discussed by
the late Educational Commission and in commenting upon it
though the Government of the North-West Provinces said that
any system of public instruction suited for boys was unsuited for
girls and that the mere establishment of female schools would
not result in any increase of female education, yet I think
they underestimated the desire of the native community in this
respect. If the success of the zenana mission is any index of
that desire, the time has come when the Government should
not only advance the cause of female education by establishing
female schools for girls from funds contributed both by itself
as well as by the various local and municipal bodies in each
district, but also by a system of secular zenana teaching sub-
sidised by it and made subject to certain contributions or fees
by those who desire to avail of it. A portaion of the Countess
of Dufferin's fund employed in the cause of female education

would also on the one hand result in supplying native female pupils for medical schools, to come out as female practitioners and work among the native community more largely than at present, as well as in making European medical aid more extensively appreciated by native females than at present. Speaking on this subject at a meeting held in aid of the Countess of Dufferin's fund I said.—

" Lady Dufferin has done more for Indian women than any other Indian reformer. But in order to make her efforts fully successful it will be necessary to make all medical aid provided to Indian women consistent with their prejudices, as well as to encourage native instead of foreign agency in the work, and to direct special efforts towards the general education of Indian women. What has hitherto been done has resulted in nothing, for the efforts have been mostly spasmodic. Statistics show that out of 1 crore and 84 lakhs of females above the age of 5 years in the N. W. Provinces and Oudh, only 21,000 are able to read and write, and of these only some 10,000 are scholars, i. e. 17 in every 10,000. (The backwardness of female education is most strikingly apparent among Hindus, who in a female population of 1 crore and 58 lakhs can only boast of 10,000 girls able to read and write and of these only 3,000 are scholars.) Among Mahomedans the number is 3,500 literates and 2,500 scholars in a population of 25 lakhs, while among Christians literates are 50 per cent and scholars 28 per cent. The statistics also show that only 83 out of every 10,000 women are employed in literary professions and I would ask my audience if you are satisfied with this state of things. Improved medical aid, though very good in itself, can only be sought after if it is valued, and it will not be valued till we gave our females the wherewithal to value it. For why do we males prefer English doctors and English medicine to Native Hakims and Baids and Native medicine ? Simply because of our progress in education and civilization, and because these have taught us that while Native medical science has remained at a standstill, European science is keeping itself abreast of the times. Let the people, therefore, make persistent efforts in the cause of female education and the Government will meet them half way". It is true that since the above words were spoken, a number of native ladies have taken the highest academical honours at Indian universities, and the Calcutta University alone has sent out some lady graduates and many undergraduates during the last 5 years. But the mass of native women is much in the same as or a slightly better condition than before as regards their education and the number of women capable of reading and writing has, as the present census would show, not so largely increased as is desirable. For this purpose the adoption of the measures above suggested is most necessary, for it is not the number of the highly educated few but of moderately educated many that determines the general intelligence of a community. In England the higher education of women is of very modern growth and it is only of late that schools for high education of girls have been established in places like Cheltenham, or that the Universities have opened their academical honours for women. But even before this system of high education was introduced or recognized in England, the number of women capable of reading and writing was very large and the number of women who exercised influence upon the affairs of their country very considerable. It was also the same in both ancient and medieval India' and there too, while women like Gargi and Maitreyi could show the highest skill in learning, the number of women capable of reading and writing was very large.* Therefore unless both the Government and the natives, especially the educated section of them, recognize in practice, as they do in theory, the importance of vastly increasing the sphere of female education by some of the methods indicated above, the question of social reform will have to wait long before it is solved. The slow progress of female education lies also at the root of the difficulty in the way of putting a stop to early or infant marriages or the more increased introduction of measures calculated to relieve the miseries of the Hindu widow.

No doubt there are difficulties in the way of this progress of female education, caused by the system of purdah on the one hand and that of early marriages

---

*In the Sankaradigvijayah we read of Sarasvati the wife of Mandan Misra having acted as arbitrator in her husband's controversy with Shankracharya and having put to him questions which no male disputant could have ever put to the great Vedantin.

on the other, but the existence of these difficulties should not deter the Government from granting those facilities for the increase of female education which it is in their power to grant. If as the Education Commission admitted, the intelligence of the women of India was far in advance of their means of obtaining school instruction and promised well for their education in future, ought not the Government to do all it can to improve those opportunities, and give a proper direction to the desire of the native community in this respect? One of the measures of operation suggested by the Indian Social Conference is a system of pledges whereby the members shall pledge themselves to educate all their women to a certain standard. But might it not be asked what facilities are there for those who take this pledge for educating their females, unless each individual himself acts as the teacher of his wife or daughter or calls in the zenana missionaries which is not always possible. If the Government had not taken the initiative in male education because of the then existing prejudices of the native community in this respect, the latter would not have made the progress it has since done. The same applies to female education and the time has come for a more decided step in this direction on the part of Government.

(2) EARLY MARRIAGES.

The other methods of raising the position of Indian women

History of early marriages.

would seem to resolve themselves into, first, the education of public opinion, whether it be by means of social conferences or the publication of social reform literature or the employment of preachers on social reform, and, second, into that of reform in the system of infant and early marriages and the removal of the prohibition of the remarriage of at least virgin widows. The former needs no comment and I shall therefore pass on to the latter giving the history of the two institutions, their effect upon the well-being of the Hindu community and if they are evil, the best means of removing them. The Hindu law as well as the Hindu religion alike regard marriage more in the nature of a sacrament than a mere contract. The young student is required to perform the ceremony of ablution in token of his having finished his course of study at his preceptor's house before entering the married state. His course of study according to Manu† ought at the earliest to take from 12 to as much as 24 years. The Smirti writers also show that the lowest permissible age was 18, and that early marriages were no part of the system of the ancient Hindus. For girls also the age of marriage was neither eight nor nine nor ten but much later, for in the Vedas and the Sutras we read of no woman being given away without her consent, which could never be given at these early ages. The marriage ritual which is as follows speaks for itself. It has as the quotation will show, no place for the girl's father after the Kanyadan ceremony. The subsequent rite is entirely an affair of the husband and wife. The mutual promises and assurances of love and protection and obedience, pre-suppose a much greater capacity in both than can be attributed to

---

† Manu, Dharmashastra (Book III. 4.)

them in their childhood. The marriage rite is no doubt a sacrament, but a sacrament which pre-supposes the age of discretion on both sides.

Seven small heaps of rice are placed at small distances, in the north-east direction. The bride-groom takes the hand of the bride and as she places her foot on the first heap says to her, "Take the first step and become the partner of my drink." Then he says, "Take the second step and become the partner of my food." "Take the third step and become the partner of my wealth and prosperity." "Take the fourth step and become the partner of my good health." "Take the fifth step and become the partner of my cattle." "Take the sixth step and become my companion in all the seasons." "Take the seventh step and become my friend."

The bride-groom continues "I take thy hand that thou mayest live with me as thy husband for a long time; the gods Bhaga, Aryama, Savita and Purandhi have given thee to me that I may be a house-holder." He says that the god Soma gave her to Gandharva, Gandharva gave her to Agni and Agni gave her to him together with wealth and sons. The bridegroom again tells the bride, " As in the word *Sáma* the syllables *Sá* and *ama* are mutually connected and interdependent, so are we; I am *ama*, thou art *Sá*. I am the heavens, thou art the earth. As a Sá ma verse is related to Rik of which it is composed so am I to thee; then shouldst thou follow me." " Like these pairs, let us marry, produce progeny, obtain sons; may they be many and may they live long."

At the conclusion of the ceremony the bridegroom and the bride say " May Prajapati bestow on us children; may Aryaman keep us united till old age. May all the gods unite our hearts; may Matarisvan and Dhatri and the goddess of speech unite us together". (Rigveda 10, 85). Either this ritual is unmeaning, as it unfortunately now is, or it involves the husband and wife being both able to understand what they were doing. A general view of all the Smirti writers moreover shows that twelve years is the safest limit of marriage- able age for girls and 16 for boys.

In the Epic period also the accounts of the Swayamvaras of Sita, Draupadi, Damayanti, Savitri and others show that early marriages were not recognized as necessary and that girls were allowed to select their own husbands. It is only in the period that followed, that injunctions regarding early marriages are first met with, though even then it was inculcated that a girl should wait for three years after her menses have appeared and then give herself away in marriage to a person of equal caste. In the Institutes of Manu * it was laid down that a girl had rather be kept unmarried the whole of her life than be given to an unsuitable person, but the usual practice was to marry girls after the age of puberty. It is in the Puranic age that the custom of early marriages came into full force and texts † like the one that the guardian of a girl who has not given her in

---

* Manu Book IX. 89.
† Prasara B. I. 64,

marriage when her menses appear, is guilty of causing miscarriage were given the force of religion. The reason why this was done lay, as I have already stated, in the neglect of the study of Sanskrit learning by the laity, in the devastation of the country by foreign invaders, in the rise of Buddhism with its horror of female charms, in the isolation of India from the rest of the world, as well as in the isolation of India's one part from another which till the introduction of steamships, railways and telegraphs, kept the Hindu's knowledge of the world much where it was. Indeed so complete was the absence of all friction of thought and opinion, so great the power of caste and custom, that Mahomedanism also partly succumbed to Hindu influence, and early marriage, prohibition of re-marriage of widows, and many other Hindu practices, are as religiously observed by certain classes of Mahomedans as if they formed part of the Koran. To the Hindu, custom became everything, the highest and the lowest were bound by it, and from its authority there was no appeal. It was hard to change it, especially where apathy and listlessness superinduced by climate made let-alone-ism the characteristic of the people. There is no other reason for such absurdities having come to be believed in by a people who boasted of such a glorious past, such a rich literature, such subtle philosophy. The Hindu is, moreover, eminently religious. His religion is a living force with him, and always keeps him company—eating, drinking, sleeping or waking, he is bound up in his religion. A people so eminently religious it would be difficult to find. The Hindu's religious teacher, the Brahman knew this, and taking advantage of it, gave any precept he wished to enforce the sanction of religion and appealed to his disciple's ideas of reward and punishment hereafter, with the result that the latter came to believe without questioning or troubling himself about the precept being ever so contrary to commonsense. The national mind, having thus been crushed and enslaved under these and other repressive influences, lost all power to question the validity of religious precepts.

The loss of national energy, the weakening of the race,

The evil effects of the custom. premature births and premature deaths, the neglect of studies, the rise of a race of weaklings, and young widows leading a life of misery, are all more or less due to this practice of infant marriages. The statistics collected at the Census of 1881 showed how widely the practice prevails throughout the country, for out of a total population of about one crore and 90 lacs of boys between the ages of one and ten, more than 6 lacs, and out of a total population of about 2 crores of girls, between the same ages 19 lacs were married, and that out of these 19 lacs 63,000 girls were widows. Between the ages of ten and fourteen the number of married girls was 44 lacs, of whom 1¾ lacs were widows, and the percentage in all cases is highest in Bengal with its 5½ per cent of boys and its 14 per cent of girls married between the ages of one and ten. In the North-West Provinces and Oudh the figures are as follows :—

1 to 9 years of age married.	Males	Females.
General population	1,27,821	2,90,700
Hindus	1,17,639	2,54,168
Mahomedans	10,088	26,328

10 to 14 years of age married.

General population..................... 6,01,526   11,64,564

Hindus................................. 5,44,501   10,36,952

Mahomedans 55,920   1,25,515

Widowers and Widows.

1 to 9 years of age.

General population 4,449   4,673

Hindus................................. 3,957   4,157

Mahomedans 482   499

10 to 14 years of age.

General population 21,941   23,593

Hindus 19,481   21,417

Mahomedans 2,398   2,113

15 to 19 years age.

General population 42,988   42,260

Hindus 37,981   37,797

Mahomedans........................... 4,908   4,308

The figures, moreover, show that among Hindus 44 in a thousand, and amongst Mohamedans 24 in a thousand, are married between the ages of 1 and 9, whilst between the ages of 10 and 15 the number is 220 in a thousand for Hindus and 147 in a thousand amongst Mohamedans. The proportion of child-widows between 1 and 20 is somewhat larger than the proportion of boy-widowers, because many a girl is married to elderly men, often of the age of 40 and upwards. The same Census report also tells us that while not one in a hundred boys is married in England between the ages of 1 and 15, about half of them are married in the North-Western Provinces and Oudh, and whilst out of a 100 females of the age of 20 and upwards, 29.55 were widows in those Provinces only 13.60 were widows in England. Up to the age of fifteen no English girl could be a widow nor an English lad a widower, and between the ages of 15 and 20 only 40 per cent of boy-husbands and 47.5 per cent of women have but a remote chance of widowhood with no prohibition of remarriage, whilst in the N.-W. Provinces as many as *seventy thousand girls*, the majority of whom are Hindus, have all the miseries of life-long widowhood to bear, without any prospect of bettering their condition. The figures also show that infant marriages prevail amongst certain classes of Mahomedans, and those too not altogether the very poorest.

But for the influence of modern education these evils would never have been recognized in the way they have now been done, and not the poor, the reckless or the degraded by vice only, but the careful, the frugal and the virtuous also would have long continued to be the victims of customs which have been sapping the energies of the race for such a long period.

Now as regards those who in spite of the too apparent dete-

Defence of the present custom and its answer.

rioration of the race as well as of the many evils caused by early marriages in the shape of many a girl-wife dying during her first confinement or losing her husband before she has come to know even the very meaning of the word *marriage* or *husband*, defend the institution of early marriages, I need only say that they are defending a hopeless case, and that whether they belong to the priestly class or to the uneducated section of the laity, or to people claiming to be educated and professing to set a higher ideal of life to their fellow subjects, they are shutting their eyes to proved facts. The teachings of later writers remarkable only for their narrow-mindedness, the influence of climate, early puberty, the requirements of caste "the etherial pleasures, of happy boy husband-hood and happy girl wife-hood,"" the spectacle of domestic peace and quiet presented by a Hindu family with its wife devoted to her husband and her husband's family, the husband devoted to his wife and children as contrasted with the divorce and other matrimonial scandals of European nations:"—these and many other arguments which are cited in favor of early and infant marrages, hold no ground now-a-days. The teachings of the later Hindu writers who sanction such marriages are not at all in accordance with the oldest and most respected authorities on Hindu law and custom as has been shown above. In addition to this the teachings of these later writers were directed to a particular state of society which if it existed when they wrote, does not exist now, under the present regime of progress and toleration. As regards climate, this does not at all require marriages to be celebrated at so early an age as is now-a-days customary. Early pubescence is also no ground, for medical testimony has proved that this early pubescence is caused by high and luxurious living, by the too early seeing and knowing of each other on the part of child-husbands and child-wives, as well as by the anxiety of parents to see their sons and daughters-in-law become fathers and mothers at an early age*. The argument that early marriage conduces to "happy

---

* The statistics collected by Dr. Tilt show that in hot climates 13·9 and in temperate climates 14. 94 is the mean age of female puberty; thus showing that marriage of girls, before 12 is opposed to all medical testimony.

husbandhood and happy wifehood" as well that the peace and quiet of a Hindu family contrast with the divorce and other matrimonial scandals of European nations has either no force or if it has any, it has none in regard to infant marriages, nor is it a sufficiently compensating force against that deterioration and weakening of the Hindus or that propogation of a race of weaklings which is now steadily going on in that society. "The divorce and other matrimonial scandals of European society" do not it is true exist in this country and it would be a terrible misfortune if ever they came to disturb the peace or happiness of Hindu society, especially as a result of the influence of European civilization. But knowing from personal experience, I think the number of happy husbands and happy wives among persons who do not marry when infants is perhaps larger in Europe than among those those who do so. My visit to England has also convinced me of the fact that in spite of all their divorce and other scandals, the number of happy husbands and happy wives in the great middle class would not compare unfavourably with the number of happy husbands and happy wives in Hindu society, with probably a greater advantage in favor of the former in the shape of increased intelligence and sounder constitutions being brought to bear upon domestic management as well as the care of children. And even if European society is cursed by these scandals, yet when the intelligence and advancement of that society are held up even by its detractors to be two out of the other advantages it possesses over Indian society, there is no reason why the latter should not profit by its brighter side leaving out the darker side, and the more so when such a course would make its approach to its own ideals nearer than its present practices. The number of women who exercise their influence on the affairs of their country in Europe is very large and wherever I met a lady of intelligence and culture I left her after feeling myself a better man. I happened to attend a meeting held in St. James's Hall in Regent Street to found a library for the parish of Marylebone, and although I had the previlege of hearing scientists like Professor Huxley and Dr. Richardson, I confess the speech of the evening to my mind was the graceful little speech of Lady John Manners. It is not in the reports of divorce court scandals or sensational novels alone that English society is faithfully described. One must know it in its every-day affairs to realize its true character. The argument that because European society is bad, therefore we should not reform, is accordingly to my mind utterly groundless.

Our marriage customs being therefore a source of great

Reform in marriage customs and methods of operation.

national injury and likely to accelerate the deterioration of our community, the question for all who are interested in the well-being of Indian society ought to be how they can be reformed. Of the great importance of female education in all questions of reform I have already spoken. Here I would only add that along with the education of our females much greater progress in the education of our males is necessary, in the direction of removing erroneous ideas like the above as well as of recognising the pernicious character of the present customs and that how entirely are they opposed to our best traditions. Without this no legislation, unless it is of the very harshest penal character, will have any effect upon the community in putting a stop to early marriages. This is being slowly done by means of lectures, debates and pamphlets, published both in English and the vernaculars, but above all by the various social reform associations now formed and are in process of being formed throughout the country. The interest shewn in the proceedings of the last three social conferences held in Allahabad, Bombay and Calcutta shows that the opposition is not from the less enlightened, many of whose minds are open to conviction, but from the educated but prejudiced few who oppose for the sake of opposition, who have yet to realize the vast issues at stake in the solution of these questions, or who from mistaken ideas of religion think the Hindu religion to be opposed to these reforms. The class of people who are unable to put down their foot upon these customs even though they are convinced of their pernicious character, is represented either by those who are wanting in the courage of their convictions and for whom caste customs and family influences are stronger than ideas of reform or by those who would make let-alone-ism their motto. That both these classes are in the wrong needs little to show and if the following quotation from a writer they so much respect does not make the scales drop from their eyes nothing else will. As to the masses, they naturally enough follow their leaders and I hope the latter will be convinced of the baneful nature of the present customs from what Herbert Spencer says of early marriages.

" In all creatures of high type, it is only when individual growth and development are nearly complete, that the production of new inidviduals becomes possible ; and the power of producing and bringing up new individuals is measured by the amount of vital power in excess of that needful for self-maintenance. The reproductive instincts, and all their accompanying emotions, become dominant when the demands for individual evolution are diminishing, and there is arising a surplus of energy which makes possible the rearing of offspring as well as the preservation of self; and speaking generally, these instincts and emotions are strong in proportion as this surplus vital energy is great. But to have a large surplus of vital energy implies a good organization—an organization likely to last long. So that in fact the superiority of physique which is accompanied by the strength of the instincts and emotions causing marriage, is a superiority of *physique* also conducive to longevity." *

Therefore nothing can be more imperative than the duty which every educated Hindu owes to himself as well as to his education, to do his utmost to put down these practices in his own family and if he shows a little courage in doing so, I am sure that he will in most cases be successful. It was said by Sherring in speaking of the educated Hindus that although they have knowledge they have " little or no conviction, no strength of character, no resolution, no clear perception and no consciousness that increased knowledge implies increased responsibility."

But though the Christian missionary was right in much of what he said, yet he failed to notice the exact nature of the difficulty under which the educated Hindu labours. It is not that the latter does not sympathize with the cause of reform,

---

* Study of Sociology, pages 94 and 95.

but the difficulties in his way are as great as in the way of those who would put down their foot upon any established usage or custom elsewhere. Even in England the censorship of custom is strong enough to thwart many a reformer and much more so may it be expected to be in India where custom has long been everything. Yet unless a beginning is made the end will never come, and the best persons to make such a beginning are those who claim to be more educated than their fellow-countrymen. The gradual raising of the marriageable age among a few families of the leaders of the community would soon have a most salutary effect and in cases where it has been attempted, as by the writer himself in his own family, the opposition has not been very great. Infant or early marriage is more in the nature of a luxury than a necessity and even the injunctions of the Shastras are made to give way to want of means. An early marriage means so much drain upon the resources of the parents of both the bride and the bridegroom, especially the former, so much so that in some communities of the Hindus in Upper India for instance in certain sections of the Kayasths as well as in other castes, where large dowries are demanded by bridegrooms at marriages, girls remain unmarried long after they have reached the age of puberty. The reform in the present system if wisely attempted is therefore not likely to lead to any serious opposition even from the more orthodox portion of the community.

One of the suggestions thrown out by the party of reform is that the Universities should, a few years hence, exclude married candidates from their matriculation examinations. This was, in fact, the practice for more than six centuries in the University of Paris which used to refuse to admit a married man into any of its faculties and insisted upon a candidate for the degree of Bachelor of Arts declaring on oath that he was unmarried.[†] In India also, as I have already shown, the gates of learning were opened only to a brahmchari (unmarried student) and many are the injunctions in the Vedas regarding the unmarried life being the only life fit for imparting the highest knowledge. The Indian Universities, now that the community itself is gradually coming to recognize the evils of early marriages, may also give further impetus to the cause of reform by ruling that, say five, or ten years hence, married boys shall not be eligible for their matriculation examinations. This will have a more beneficial effect in postponing many a marriage of both boys and girls than even the present amendment of the law relating to the age of consent.

Another pernicious result of the institution of early marriages is the addition to the already increasing population of this country of a number of weaklings without any corresponding increase in their means of subsistence. It is true that marriage among Hindus is a sacrament and the procreation of a son one of the most meritorious acts which a Hindu can perform, but even the Hindu Shastras never sanctioned marriage before a man was able to support a family, and the writer of these Shastras clearly laid down that marriage was to be performed after a man had completed his studies and

Increase of population without increase of the means of subsistence as a result of early marriages.

[†] P. Montegazza; Hygiene de l'amour, p. 231.

learnt something wherewith to maintain a family. This however is not now the practice and considering our over-crowded population and the prevalence of misery bordering upon starvation, the question may well be asked whether the preventative check of not marrying early is one that should be impressed upon the minds of the people as largely as the other advantages to be gained from deferring marriage. In some countries of Europe the prevalence of misery among the poorer classes has made this question one of practical politics. In England there is often a general disinclination to marry even among those who could otherwise afford to maintain a family. In Norway and parts of Switzerland the labouring classes knowing that by having large families they will sink below the condition of comfort to which they have been accustomed, refrain from rash and early marriages. In some other countries of Europe Mal thus says it is the practice of the state to forbid a marriage unless a man can show that he could support a family. In Thibet also celibacy is deemed honourable while marriage is almost a certain bar to a man rising in the state. The ancient lawgivers of Greece, as Plato, Solon and Aristotle, all laid it down as one of the duties of the state to allow men and women to procreate children only when at their greatest vigour. In India on the other hand the case is quite different. Men and women—or rather boys and girls—are here married at the earliest age possible and procreate children at an age when in other countries they would be in the school-room, adding prematurely to an already starving population. The mass of the Indian people are now unable to withstand even a single bad season, and population has so largely increased, that there is much greater poverty than before and food reserves have been greatly depleted. In times gone by, on the other hand, the population was not so large as now, and the food reserves of the people enabled them to withstand the effects of a bad season longer than at present. The Government of the day had no foreign exports of grain nor an increasingly large mass of paupers to support. Wild beasts, in the shape of tigers, leopards and wolves as well as men coming from the north or forming themselves into gangs in India itself, kept the increase of population in check. This is not possible now, and the question as to how this large mass of population could be saved from death and starvation, naturally forces itself upon public attention. Famines and scarcities are no longer abnormal states of the masses in India, and, this being so, they ought to occupy that attention on the part of the Government which they deserve. The growing danger to this country is that it has to feed, in 1891, $6\frac{1}{2}$ percent more people than in 1881. Now, it was pointed out by the Famine Commission that in Bengal 24 millions of people are struggling to live upon 15 million acres. In the North-Western Provinces, it was a little better ten years ago, for out of a total population of 44 millions, 30 millions were estimated to derive their subsistence from $34\frac{1}{2}$ million acres under cultivation. Unless the fifteen million acres, which are returned as culturable, have since been brought under cultivation, the increase of population in the North-Western Provinces at the above rate would, five years hence, cause the struggle there to be nearly as hard as it is in the more thickly populated parts of India. The Indian ryot will not leave his village, if he can help it. In fact he will suffer every hardship rather than leave his homestead. Migrations from the more densely to the less densely populated parts of India cannot, therefore, be expected to take place on any large scale within the next few years, nor will people migrate into Native States because of their Governments not being good. Although, therefore, the country may have plenty of land for its increasing population, yet the pressure of population will always be great in its more densely populated districts. The situation is thus alarming and neither improved government nor plans of emigration, nor any benevolent institutions, nor any degree or direction of industry can take the place of that moral check on population, namely, the asking of the question whether one ought to marry without the means of supporting children. If the Indian labourer or the agriculturist would only refrain from marrying till he was able to support a family, much of his squalid poverty would be removed. There are few things which tend so largely to diminish human happiness as marrying without the means of supporting children. And unless the Indian agriculturist or labourer himself realizes the fact that he himself is the cause of his own poverty; that the means of improving his condition are in his own hands ; that society and Government, however they may desire to assist him, cannot do so of themselves; that when the wages of his labour will not support a family, it is a sign that the country cannot support more inhabitants; and that by marrying early he is throwing a useless burden upon society and plunging himself into distress, misery, and disease, no suggestion for reform will improve his condition.

In all cases he should put to himself the question whether his son whom he is going to marry, has the adequate means of supporting a wife. He should learn that bodily and mental vigor achieves success and bodily and mental weakness leads to failure in life, that to begin early is to end early, that the children of late marriages are healthier, stronger and live longer than the children of early marriages, that the latter deprive a man of his independence, destroy all enterprise and reduce him to the necessity of depending upon any pittance he can get and that no Government could help him until he helps himself.

The last remedy is legislation, upon which there is necessarily much difference of opinion. For this is

Legislation in the matter of early marriages.

a remedy which ought never to be adopted (especially in a country like India where the rulers, though they profess a different religion from the ruled, yet allow complete religious freedom to the latter), except it be for the removal of practices or customs repugnant to humanity or unless those practices are represented by a considerable section of the subject community to be such as cannot be removed without the intervention of the Legislature. This has been the line hitherto followed by the Indian Legislature and this was also the reply given by the Indian Government after reviewing the whole question both in 1886, * as well as in 1891.

---

* The Government Resolution, No. 35. 1616- 26, dated 8th October, 1886, was as follows.—

"In dealing with such subjects as those raised in Mr. Malabari's Notes, the British Government in India has usually been guided by certain

I am myself not in favor of forced legislation in social matters and am in full sympathy with those who think that

general principles. For instance, when caste or custom enjoins a practice which involves a breach of the ordinary criminal law, the State will enforce the law. When caste or custom lays down a rule which is of its nature enforceable in the Civil Courts, but is clearly opposed to morality or public policy, the State will decline to enforce it. When caste or custom lays down a rule which deals with such matters as are usually left to the option of citizens, and which does not need the aid of Civil or Criminal Courts for its enforcement, State interference is not considered either desirable or expedient.

In the application of such general principles to particular cases, there is doubtless room for differences of opinion, but there is one commonsense test which may often be applied with advantage in considering whether the State should or should not interfere in its legislative or executive capacity with social or religious questions of the kind now under notice. The test is, " Can the State give effect to its commands by the ordinary machinery at its disposal ?" If not, it is desirable that the State should abstain from making a rule which it cannot enforce without a departure from its usual practice or procedure.

If the test be applied in the present case, the reasons will be apparent why His Excellency in Council considers that interference by the State is undesirable, and that the reforms advocated by Mr. Malabari, which affect the social customs of many races with probably as many points of difference as of agreement, must be left to the improving influences of time, and to the gradual operation of the mental and moral development of the people by the spread of education.

It is truethat the British Government in India has by its legislation set up a standard of morality independent of, and in some material respects differing from, the standard set up by caste, and it may be that the former standard has had some beneficial effect in influencing native customs, practices and modes of thought. But legislation, though it may be didactic in its effects, should not be undertaken for merely didactic purposes; and in the competition of influence between legislation, on the one hand, and caste or custom on the other, the condition of success on the part of the former is that the Legislature should keep within its natural boundaries, and should not by overstepping those boundaries, place itself in direct antagonism to social opinion".

The community ought itself to reform its social institutions rather than invoke the aid of the Legislature, especially when it is the Legislature of a Government foreign to the people. What ought, however, to be guarded against is prejudice, whether it be in favor of or against Government interference. No society can be prosperous because of its actions being everywhere regulated by artificial agencies, or by a multiplication of laws. Such laws seldom produce the direct effects intended and produce many indirect effects that were never contemplated by the framers or the invokers of those laws. The feeling against Government interference is thus a healthy feeling. But it should not be allowed to stand in the way of legitimate interference, or to perpetuate evils under the mistaken belief that a society had better suffer some evils rather than go to its rulers for legislation. On the contrary the true principle that ought to guide the community in such matters is whether the opinions of Government are the opinions of its people, whether their power is the power of the people, and whether the matter is one which is within the sphere of legal control or whether the Government represents in the particular matter proposed for legislation interests opposed to those of the community.

Acting upon these principles I shall proceed to show how far the question of early marriages falls within the legitimate sphere of legislation. The Legislature cannot step forward to make early or infant marriages penal—nor, as has been proposed, could it consistently with its own policy of religious toleration, say that a Hindu boy or girl married during infancy could, by making a declaration before a magistrate, repudiate his or her marriage. Such a law would overstep all bounds of legitimate legislative action as well as overturn the whole of the Hindu society. Marriage under the Hindu law is not a mere contract but a sacrament and could not be dissolved by an act of the law as in other communities. Says Manu "Never let (a woman) wish to separate herself from her father, her husband, or her sons ; for, by a separation from them she exposes both families to contempt. Him to whom her father has given her, or her brother with the paternal assent, let her obsequiously honor, while he lives ; and when he dies, let her never neglect him."*

She, who deserts not her lord but keeps in subjection to him her heart, her speech and her body, shall attain his mansion in heaven, and, by the virtuous in this world be called *Sàdhevi or good and faithful.* But a wife by disloyalty to her husband shall incur disgrace in this life, and be born in the next from the womb of a shakal, or be tormented with horrible diseases which punish vice.†

The other Smirti writers are also as explicit as Manu upon the duties of women towards their husbands. Says Hárita " The wife is the home : a man should not consider his home a habitation ungraced by a wife ; therefore is she another home."

Regarding husbands also the injunctions of Manu are very plain in enjoining mutual fidelity till death and the only case where a wife could be deserted is that of barrenness or bad temper. On the other hand to send a virtuous wife adrift in the world is nowhere recognized or sanctioned in the

---

* Manu Chapter V. 149 and 151.

† Ibid Chapter IX. 29 and 30.

Shastras. Says Apastamba "He who has unjustly forsaken his wife shall put on an ass's skin, with the hair turned outside, and beg in seven houses, saying give alms to him who forsook his wife."

Therefore to sanction the repudiation of marriage by either husband or wife when they come of age will revolutionize the whole social fabric of the Hindus. The marriage contract when once made is, under the Hindu law, irrevocable and the courts have also unanimously held that a marriage once duly solemnized cannot be set aside except on the ground of fraud, so much so that the doctrine of *factum valet* has been applied to Hindu marriages both on the ground of religious theory and social difficulty. Such a law, as proposed, would, therefore, involve serious interference with the domestic life of the Hindus and is not one that will put a stop to early marriages. Public opinion will never sanction such an interference on the part of the Legislature and I fully recognize the unwillingness of Government to embark on a change so repugnant to the feelings of the Hindus.

Another suggestion that has been made is that parents may, by law, be enabled to defer the marriage of their children to any age they like and that all overt acts on the part of their neighbours or castemen be made punishable as public offences or contempts of courts.

There is, however, at present nothing to prevent a Hindu father and mother from deferring the marriage of their child to any age they like, and so far as Upper India is concerned, no excommunication or any other overt act is done by the neighbours or castemen against the person who keeps his son or daughter unmarried after he or she has attained the age of puberty. On the contrary, while custom in a manner forces a parent to follow the rules of his caste in regard to the marriage of his children, so far as I know, no formal excommunication follows if he disobeys the custom. Even, therefore, if the Legislature were to interfere and pass the proposed law its interference will not put a stop to infant or early marriages, for custom will still retain its stronghold as effectually upon individuals after the passing of the proposed law as it does now. No law can punish a community for bringing its moral or social influence to bear upon one of its members in marrying his children at a particular age and even if overt acts of excommunication and other disabilities inflicted by such community were made punishable by law, the latter could not force its members to eat, drink, associate or contract marriage relations with a person whom they think guilty of breaking its rules, which for the party concerned is as effectual as any formal excommunication.

The laws of all civilized countries, however, have fixed the age at which a marriage could be legal. Legislation in fixing the marriageable age. In almost all European countries 18 for boys and between 12 and 14 for girls is the minimum marriageable age fixed by law. In India also the ancient law-givers fixed the marriageable age both for boys and girls, and I think that if the State were to rule by civil enactment that marriages below a certain age shall not be valid for civil purposes, it will not be violating its principles of religious neutrality nor forcing its own innovations upon Hindu society ; 11 or 12 years for girls and 14 or 15 for boys if fixed as the minimum ages, would be in accordance with the practices of many sections of the community. This is not at all a matter of religious interference. For infant marriage has, as I have above shown, no connection with religion in the sense this word ought to be properly understood. If it has any connection, it has with custom which by long usage is looked upon by some as having the force of religion, but which by as many more is repudiated without their being any the worse for it. If customs, which have come to be regarded as associated with religion, are always to be respected by Government with extreme scrupulousness, Suttee would not have been abolished, nor obscene singing and insulting people in the streets on certain festivals put a stop to, nor the marriage of widows legalized, nor a Hindu who had renounced the religion of his forefathers declared, contrary to the express injunctions of Hindu law, entitled to inherit his ancestral property, nor of all others, a Hindu widow guilty of unchastity held not to have forfeited her late husband's estate, though Hindu opinion, Hindu law and Hindu religion are all opposed to it. If humanity and the altered conditions of Native society dictated these laws, the same things necessitate the alteration of the present law of marriage, which is ruining the Hindu nation. While, therefore, it is the plain duty of all educated Hindus to set themselves about reforming this custom of early marriage in their own families and communities, it is also their duty to move the Legislature in the way proposed. Such a law would be quite consonant with public feeling. It would also be in accordance with the practices of many sections of the Hindu community, and if registrations of births and deaths under Act **VI.** of 1886 were made with care and accuracy, all fears of litigation arising on account of disputes regarding the age at which a marriage took place shall be removed. This could, however, only be done on the motion of a considerable section of the Hindu community itself and the best way of doing it is, either for the Government to appoint a Commission to take the sense of the Hindu community in this respect, or for a body like the Social Conference to move the Government in this behalf.

Another much debated subject is the amendment of the law regarding suits for restitution of conjugal rights. Whatever may be the origin of the English law on the subject, such suits have been entertained (in the courts of British India for a long course of years. The Hindu law as now interpreted provides for the entertainment of such suits by the courts under texts like the following " A husband who abandons an affectionate wife, or her who speaks not harshly, who is sensible, constant and faithful, shall be brought to his duty by the king with a severe chastisement." *

Amendment of the law with respect to suits for restitution of conjugal rights.

" If a wife legally superseded shall depart in wrath {from the house, she must either instantly be confined, or abandoned in the presence of the whole family."† Following these and other similar rules of the Hindu law, it has been ruled that the main rights and duties of the husband and wife are *inter se* legal as distinct from moral rights and duties, and their

---

* Narada's Institutes.

† Manu—Chapter IX. 83.

enforcement devolves upon the king. . Such rights and duties could be enforced by one party against the other and not exclusively by the husband against the wife. And the Civil Courts of the British India as occupying the position in respect of judicial functions formerly occupied in the system of Hindu Law by the king, have jurisdiction in respect of the enforcement of such rights and duties.*

Such suits are, however, mostly confined to the lower classes of the Hindu community, and during some fifteen years' experience of the courts in British India I have only had one occasion to try a suit for restitution of conjugal rights between persons of the higher sections of that community. This was a suit brought by a member of a respectable Kayasth family against his wife who had left him, because of his misconduct which consisted in associating, eating and drinking openly with persons of other religions as well as of his cruelty towards her. The cruelty and miscondct having both been proved, the case was thrown out both by me as well as by all the higher courts. Since then although I have had occasion to try several suits for restitution of conjugal rights between the lower classes of Hindus viz. Jats, Gujars and others as well as between some classes of Mahomedans, I had never had occasion to try any such suit between Brahmins, Kshatryas, Vaishyas or other high castes of Hindus and I have invariably found that among those sections of the community whether Hindu or Mahomedan, which brings such suits, the marriage tie is either very loose or the woman does not belong to any

* Binda v. Kaunsilla—Allahabad High Court Weekly Notes for 1891, p. 18.

respectable family but is generally a woman of loose character who marries and leaves her husband at pleasure. In all such cases wherever a decree is given by the courts, it very often remains ineffectual by the wife leaving her husband immediately after she has been made over to him or allows her property to be attached or even suffers imprisonment rather than return to him. Any amendment of the law in this respect will not, therefore, further the cause of Social reform, nor put a stop to early marriages. Experience, moreover, tells me that in India such suits are usually prompted by spite and that even if the courts were given the option of awarding imprisonment to recusant wives or husbands or the power of limiting the term of such an imprisonment, the cause of Social reform will neither be any worse nor better for it. The present law which empowers them to entertain such suits is probably not without some deterrent effect upon the community, and I would not have it altered by the Legislature except it be to give the courts power to award imprisonment to the recusant party as they think fit as well as to limit the term of such imprisonment. It is not in British India alone that suits for restitution of conjugal rights are tried as civil suits ; on the contrary the laws of some Native States even make desertion by a husband or wife a penal offence and compel the recusant party to obedience by punishing him or her as a criminal. For instance the Indore Panal Code provides. S.''254. Whoever violates the conjugal rights of a husband or wife shall be punished with imprisonment in the house of the complainant, or if the husband does not consent to imprison the wife in his house, in the Civil Jail, if he pays for her maintenance until the offender agrees to restitute such rights or until their marriage is dissolved.   Prosecutable by the wife or husband".

When I had to administer this law a case came up before me in appeal in which it was found necessary to point out the impossibility of carrying out its provisions regarding the wife being imprisoned in her husband's house. That was a case between persons of a very low caste which I took care to ascertain allowed a wife to remarry in the life-time of a husband who had deserted her.   The husband was a weak, infirm and idiotic person who had never lived with his wife for many years, and thinking that it would be unjust to apply the penal law of the State to such a case, I declined to send the wife to be imprisoned in her husband's house or in the Jail. The case attracted some notice from the press, and while my judgment was approved of by a very large section of the community who thought I had granted to the woman in the case before me, a relief which the courts in British India had failed to grant in Rukmabai's case, the more orthodox section of the native press expressed their fear lest it be cited as a precedent in cases among the higher sections of the community.   My view of the matter is, however, the same as it was when I passed this judgment, and I think that though suits for restitution of conjugal rights whether they be brought in the courts of British India or in those of Native States, as a rule, fail to achieve their object and that the only fetters to confine a wife in her husband's house are those of love or attachment and not those of legal coercion, yet I would not have the law rescinded in the interests of the Hindu community itself. *

---

* Comp. Manu (Chap. IX, 12)

The difficulty in the way of the Indian Legislature when

Raising the age of consent. legislating upon social matters of the Hindus could not be better illustrated than by the way in which religion and the Queen's Proclamation have been cited in opposition to the present proposal to raise the age of consent under section 376 of the Indian Penal Code. The Legislature in this instance did not move only on the motion of the committee formed in England for the promotion of social reform in India, but also on the motion of the Indian people as represented by the Indian Social Conference. The measure is one dictated by motives of ordinary humanity and has for its object the protection of girls from being the victims of the passions of their husbands. It is not at all opposed to religion which, if properly understood, never enjoins sexual intercourse by a husband with his wife at even the age of 12, much less at the age of ten or eleven. The Garbhadhana ceremony which has been cited in defence of the present practice is never performed in a very large, if in any part of India. The Queen's Proclamation, which respects religious usages and institutions, does not apply to the case of husbands who ruin their wives in the name of Garbhadhana or any other religious ceremony. And yet this small measure of reform has given rise to a most violent and vehement excitement in Bengal and elsewhere as if the whole religious fabric of the Hindus was in danger of being crushed by foreign innovation. As has been pointed out by more than one Vedic scholar, the Garbhadhana ceremony is not necessarily to be performed on the first appearance of the signs of puberty and may be performed at any time.

I have also consulted the original texts on that subject and think that the Shatapatha Brahman, the Institutes of Manu, the Ashvalayana, the Gobhila and the Shaunak Grihya Sutras, show that as the object of the ceremony was to obtain a son who would do honour to his family, it could not be performed unless the father and mother were both fully developed. The way in which the various mantras are supposed to be recited by both man and wife also shows that they were both supposed to be of mature age and when, as I have shown, there were no infant or early marriages in ancient India, the Garbhadhana ceremony could not have taken place at the early age now advocated by modern writers. The Vedas contain many a prayer on the part of the father to the gods to protect the child in the womb and they unmistakeably show that the mother of the child was supposed to be a woman not of 11 or 12 years of age, but much older. The argument that the British Legislature is interfering with the religion of the Hindus therefore falls to the ground.

The Queen's Proclamation, further, does not apply to cases like this, for it is the duty of the State to protect its subjects from unjust harm, and what harm could be more unjust to a young girl than to be deprived of health and youth and, in some cases, of life also, by her so-called husband. On the other hand, if the Queen's Proclamation applies, it applies as much to the men as to the women of India, and if the former claim its protection, the latter are also entitled to do so. It is, therefore, a matter of great regret that the cry of "religion in danger" has been raised by those who owe it to their own education to support instead of opposing the Government, when it does a thing which is for their own good. If there are any defects in the measure, and that there are defects I shall presently point out, the Government may be asked to remove them ; but to condemn the measure wholesale is justified neither by reason nor by religion nor by the Queen's Proclamation.

I have made inquiries in several places about the general feeling on this vexed question and am told that though the measure is not one which would put a stop to early marriages, yet it would prevent the deterioration of Hindu girls. A Hindu lady to whom I was speaking the other day on this question exclaimed " It is only the rogue or the libertine that have sexual intercourse with a girl before 12 !" The practice of a large section of the Hindu community in Upper India is also not to let their daughters visit their husbands before they have reached the age of puberty. And the latter takes place usually after 12. In cases where the menses appear before that age, they appear either from a diseased condition of the system or from forced development. Such cases are, however, very rare and ought not to be cited in opposition to the measure. There is, however, a well-grounded fear of harassing prosecutions taking place under the new law. The public seems to have a great distrust of the police and the Magistracy, and thinks that in these days of strained feelings in order to disarm the police as well as others of their power of harassing respectable people, a provision be added to Chapter XV. of the Criminal Procedure Code to the effect that no court shall take cognizance of an offence under the first part of Section 376, I. P. C., as now amended, except upon the complaint of the girl herself, or her legally constituted guardian ; and that in case the medical examination of a girl is ordered by a Magistrate no such examination shall take place except by a female medical practitioner. It is also a general feeling prevalent among the community that to make premature sexual intercourse by a man with his own wife punishable with transportation for life or ten years imprisonment, is condemning the girl to a forced widowhood and that such a heavy punishment deprives the measure of all its educative effects. I myself fully endorse the views of the community in this respect and think that the ends of the case do not require a severer punishment than that of 2 years. Beyond suggesting these amendments I have no sympathy with the unreasonable agitation now set on foot in Bengal and elsewhere against this small measure of reform, and hope the Government will pass it, but with the above amendments. *

The next question that I shall take up is the present prohibition of inter-marriages not only between various castes but even between sections of a caste. This was not so in the early times, for Manu sanctioned for a Brahman four, for a Kshatrya three, for a Vaishya two, and

Inter-marriages.

---

* In the English law sexual intercourse by a man with his own wife is not rape and it ought not to be treated or punished as such in India. On the contrary unless it results in death or grievous hurt, it should be treated and punished as premature sexual intercourse and I think the Bill may be modified in this respect also. Its present amendment in limiting the cognizance of the offence by a Magistrate of the District or a Chief Presidency Magistrate or its investigation by an officer of the Police not below the rank of the Inspector, would scarcely meet the wishes of the community or put a stop to harrassing prosecutions.

for a Sudra one wife, in the inverse order of his caste. The Smirti writers also speak of the children of such unions. It is only in modern times that this prohibition of inter-marriages has become so strong as to be applicable not only to inter-marriage between various castes but within the various sections of a caste also. Manu only laid down that a man may marry a girl who is not of the same Gotra and who is not within the prohibited degrees both on the father and the mother's side ; he did not lay down any prohibition for a Brahman marrying in his own caste. But now-a-days a Saraswat Brahman cannot marry into the family of a Gaur Brahman, without losing caste, and *vice versa.* Among Rajputs inter-marriages among various sections of the caste are more common, and this class has thus set a most worthy example to other classes of Hindus, though even one section of this community, the Bhagel Rajputs, deems itself lowered by inter-marriage with any other section of the Rajput community. This limitation of marriage in certain castes or families has led to a most absurd custom among a section of the Brahman community called the Chaubas or more properly *Chaturvedis* (learned in the four Vedas), but who in these degenerate times are not even able to read one, to say nothing of the four Vedas. This class has a custom that on the occasion of a girl being given by one family to another, the latter will give a girl to a youth of the former. This is called *Badla* or exchange, and the obligation is enforced even up to the second and third generations, and many Chaubas who have no expectation of having girls in their families have to keep their boys unmarried in consequence. Talking to a member of this caste the other day I pointed out to him the unreasonableness of the custom, but was told in reply that unless the Sirkar did something to stop this practice it could not be stopped! In other classes of Hindus, people will take girls in marriage from, but will not give theirs to certain sections of their own castes. The result of this is that weakening of the race which must follow the selection of husbands and wives being confined within a narrow circle. It is also the fruitful cause of large dowries being demanded by bridegrooms or fathers of bridegrooms from brides' fathers, as among certain sections of Brahmans, and of people becoming involved in debt or feeling otherwise miserable, on account of having an unmarried daughter. The remedy lies in the reformers' appealing to the text of their ancient religion as well as in impressing upon the people the pernicious character of the present prohibition. Inter-marriage between various castes may not be possible, but that between the various sections of a caste especially between those which could dine together is not at all opposed to religion. It would, on the contrary, result in widening the area of selection as well as in decreasing the extortion now practised under the name of religion.

It is also a common practice in certain sections of the community to demand extortionate dowries in marriages, and the system often proves a source of much trouble to fathers of girls who have to pay such dowries. In some castes the practice is carried to the extent of the bridegroom refusing to take the bride home even after every thing else has been completed unless he is paid so

Marriage dowries.

much money in the shape of dowry, and the bride's father is often driven to either borrowing the money required or to have recourse to fraud in order to escape the extortion. In other sections of the Hindu community, girls are sold by needy parents to persons who are either entirely unfit to enter the married state or are on the brink of the grave. Such money is never received openly. Manu distinctly forbids it. Says that ancient law-giver:—

" Let the father of a girl not receive the smallest *Sulka* (consideration) in return for giving his daughter in marriage, as *Sulka* taken from covetousness betokens the sale of one's offspring. Those of a woman's sinful relatives who live upon her wealth or use her conveyances or clothes go to hell."

In the Arsha form of marriage, a pair of cows is sanctioned by some to be receiveable as Sulka. But this is wrong, a considration, whether small or large, amounts to a sale of off-spring."*

Public opinion is also opposed to the receipt of such consideration, yet young girls are often forced into matrimony to the great injury of their future prospects. Now and then, matters go to the courts and the question arises whether a marriage performed in lieu of such consideration is valid. The Chief Court of the Punjab, before whom such a question came up lately, have held that though by the custom of the Punjab, parents are vested with authority to dispose of their minor children in marriage as they consider best, the policy of the law. however, in conferring such power on parents is to secure the benefit of the minor. Whereas the object of an agreement

---

*Manu—Chap. III. 51, 52, 53.

such as that under reference is to procure, by corrupt means, the parent's or the guardian's consent to the desired marriage. The tendency of such an agreement is, therefore, to subordinate the interests of the minor to those of the guardian. Such transactions, it was held, may be common in the country, but they are not upheld by the Hindu community at large. This view was, however, not taken by the other courts in India, for the Allahabad High Court has ruled in the case of a father who wished to give his daughter in marriage to a decrepit old man in lieu of money that he could do so, and although the court sympathized with the girl and even condemned the father's action, yet they refused to grant her any protection. In a third case recently decided by the Madras High Court a girl of 4 years of age was given in marriage by her mother without the consent of the father and during his temporary absence from home. The father of the girl did not sanction the marriage and yet the court ruled that the marriage was legal. Now here are cases which are within the proper sphere of the Legislature and in which legislation will be in accordance with both the religion and the public opinion of the Hindu community. If they make the Civil Courts guardian of a minor's person and property, they should not confine such guardianship to minors having property. On the contrary they ought to save hundreds of Hindu girls from being victims of their parents' cupidity or folly by being forced into marriage with persons utterly unfit to be their husbands. Religion and public opinion alike condemn this practice, and the Legislature should not lag behind. Would it not be more proper to have a short section added to the Minors' Act to the effect that if a girl's parents are about to marry her to an unsuitable person for money or otherwise, any person interested in her may have the marriage stopped by applying to the Civil Court, which may exercise its discretion according to the circumstances, while any money that may be thus received may also be declared recoverable at the girl's suit? The dowry received by a girl's husband's father may also be declared to be her property. This would at once put a stop to the practice of demanding extortionate dowries at marriages.

(3.) THE HINDU WIDOW.

Coming now to another most painful result of early marriages and the misinterpretation of the teachings of the ancient sacred texts of the Hindus, viz. the life of celibacy which is enforced by custom upon a Hindu widow, we find that in 1881, there were not less than one crore and 61 lacs of widows among a total Hindu female population of some 8 crore and 16 lacs, and that of these not less than 63,000 were widows between the ages of one and ten and 1 lac 74,000 between those of ten and fourteen, or altogether about $2\frac{1}{3}$ lacs of girl-widows at an age at which in other countries they would be in the school-room or the nursery. The proportion of widows is the strongest among the Brahmins, being 31 percent out of the total female population of that caste, and the question is whether a community in which every fourth married woman is a widow could be otherwise than unhappy.

History of the prohibition of the remarriage of Hindu widows.

The Hindu religion as rightly interpreted never sanctioned such a life of celibacy as is now enforced upon widows, for in the Vedas we read.—

" Get up, O ! woman, thou who liest down by the side of this, thy lifeless husband. Come to this crowd of living people about thee here, and mayest thou become the wife of some person desirous of taking the hand of a widow in marriage." (Yajur Veda Taitriya Aranyaka, 6th Prapathaka, 14th Sloka). The same text occurs in the other Vedas also and is quoted by Asvalayana and Bandhayana.

" She who having had a first husband subsequently marries another second husband, provided they two give an Aja Panchodan, they should not separate". (Atharva Veda IX. 5. 27.)

" This second husband goes to the same heaven as the twice married woman, if he gives an Aja Panchodan and additional offerings to the sun." (Ibid.IX. 5. 28.)

" Such married couples after giving a cow with her calf, a bullock, a bed, clothes and gold go to the best of heavens." (Ibid IX. 5. 29).

The Smriti writers are even more explicit.—

" She (who is abandoned by her husband or is a girl-widow) if she has never cohabited with a man, is fit to be married to a second husband. If she leaves her first husband, and returns back without having cohabited with another man, the first husband may go through a second ceremony of marriage with her." (Manu IX. 175-176.)

" On the death of the husband if a girl-wife has been merely married with the recital of the Mantras, but has never cohabited with her husband, she is fit to be given in marriage again." (Vashishta 17).

" If she is a girl-widow or has been abandoned by her husband by force or violence, then she is fit to be taken as a

wife by any man upon a second ceremony of marriage."
(Prajapati).

" Even if the marriage rites have all been completed if
a girl has not cohabited with her husband, she is fit to be
married again. She is like an unmarried girl, or as though
no marriage had been celebrated." (Narada.)

In the Mahabharta also we read of Arjuna having married
Ulupi, the widowed daughter of a patriarch of the Naga
tribe and the son that was born of her was treated as a
legitimate son. Krishna the great hero's son also married
a widow, and in the Padma Purana we read of a daughter of
a king of Kashi having been married several times because
of the death of each of her husbands soon after her marriage.

The history of the change of custom in this respect is the
same as of the change in respect of early marriages viz. the
decline of the respect formerly given to women and of the
tender regard shown to them by early law-givers, the rise of a
dogmatic and superstitiously ignorant priesthood and an ignorant
laity and the isolation of the Hindus from the rest of the world.
The present texts on this prohibition of widow re-marriage are as follows.—

" But she (a widow) may at *will* (when her husband is dead)
emaciate her body by (living on) pure flowers, fruits (and)
roots. She may not, however, when her husband is dead,
mention even the name of another man.

2, " She must be till death subdued, intent, chaste, following that best (law) which is the rule of wives of a single
husband.

3. Many thousands of Brahmans, chaste from youth, have gone to heaven without leaving children to continue the family.

4. Her husband being dead, a virtuous wife, firm in chastity, goes though childless, to heaven like those chaste (men).

5. But the woman who, from desire of offspring, is unfaithful to (her dead) husband, meets with blame here, and is deprived of her husband's place (in the next world).

6. There is no offspring here begotten by another (than the husband), nor even on marrying another, nor is a second husband anywhere permitted to good women. (Manu—Chap. V. 157 to 162).

" The remarriage of a girl once married in due form, the excess portion due to the eldest brother, the killing of cows, begetting a son on a brother's wife, and becoming a Sanyási, are prohibited in Kaliyuga." (Adi Purana).

" The gift in remarriage to another of a girl once given away in marriage is prohibited in the Kaliyuga." (Brahad Naradiya Purana).

Yet in spite of these injunctions instances are not wanting where even before the advent of the British rule, Brahmans of reputed learning sought to rebel against the custom, apparently thinking that as neither Manu nor the authors of the subsequent Smritis recognized or countenanced marriages of girls in their infancy, their prohibitions were never meant to apply to virgin widows. On the contrary the very idea of *Sati, or Sadhwi i e.* a chaste or virtuous woman, implied that she was capable of understanding the meaning of the word Sati or Sadhia ; and the Hindu lawgiver himself would, if he had lived in these days, have given the same answer and appealed to his own texts in support of it.

There is some thing illogical and repugnant to common
sense in the very word—a *virgin widow*, and a continuance of customs which force upon such a widow the life of a Brahmacharni before she is able to understand what such a life means, could only be due to a misinterpretation of the ancient religious texts of the Hindus. The very presence of a widow in a family casts a gloom upon every joyous occasion and the younger she is the greater is the gloom in the family, and no greater insult can be afforded to a woman than to call her a widow. The doctrine of previous karma which is so strongly urged in defence of the practice does not apparently apply, for the inculcators of that doctrine have throughout their teachings also said that one could by exertion in this life avert the evil consequences of his acts in the past, which situated as she is, a virgin widow could not. Poets have denounced and the victims of the custom have themselves appealed to the public against, their cruel fate, but not with much result. Well might a Hindu widow say to the Almighty in the words of the poet " I have tasted the bitterness of a living death for many years, I have been consumed in a burning fire all my days. My dead husband was not only reduced to ashes himself, but left me to the misery of a continual burning. I have not known what happiness is. May I forget all my griefs in Thee. May

Life of a Hindu widow and present aspect of the custom.

I forget all that have been near and dear to me and mayest Thou be in my heart as well as upon my lips."

But it is asked do the sufferers from this custom really require our aid, and is it not a fact that sympathy, care, watchfulness and the tenderest desire to mitigate as far as possible the lot of the poor widow, combined with religious precepts and teaching, like those mentioned above, and the general seclusion of females, have all tended to keep Hindu widows purer than might have been otherwise expected. Does not many a widow prove " a perfect woman nobly planned," and realize the truth of the saying that present trials are but the seeds of future glories and ought not fasts, penances, religious and charitable duties, to make up the sum total of her existence ? In the coldest season of the year she would go to the local river or tank for her morning ablutions. In the rains she would abstain from food on alternate days or give up such necessary articles of diet as salt, condiments &c. and often live upon only one meal a day or giving up all cooked food and follow Manu's texts by living on pure roots and fruits.

Her relatives instead of being cruel or unkind to her or anxious to get her property, if she is childless, often induce her to adopt a son to perpetuate her husband's family or raise a sum towards her maintenance. In some classes custom forces them to do so whether she is rich or poor. As she gains experience she assumes the position of the family matron and her authority is supreme in all domestic matters. She is no more a household drudge than any other woman of the family, whose husband is alive and her presence is not everywhere unwelcome at family festivities. The same custom, therefore, which prohibits her remarriage, has also done all that it could to mitigate her hardships. But while I fully admit the truth of all these remarks and think it highly creditable to the high sense of morality that prevails among our women that so many of them have successfully proved themselves true martyrs to custom, yet the fact must also not be forgotten that much immorality and a large number of foeticides and infanticides as well as a very large proportion of females of loose character are due to this prohibition of the remarriage of widows. With many widows there is often a positive disinclination to remarry, not only among Hindus but also among classes which sanction remarriage. But cases in which Nature, though kept down by custom and tradition, breaks out and asserts herself, are not rare and we should not be quite beyond the mark in saying that not a few prostitutes in our large towns come from women who once belonged to respectable families, whom custom kept back from remarrying and who broke through all restraints and brought dishonour upon themselves and their families. When one of these elopements occurs, the Hindu society of the place is convulsed for the moment, but public conscience soon goes to sleep in the belief that it is useless to fight against fate.

The fact is that this prohibition of the remarriage of at least virgin widows is an unmixed evil and a dark spot upon the domestic life of the Hindus and it should be the anxious care of every Hindu to ameliorate it.

The British law has given the Hindu widow liberty to

Reforms in the present customs. remarry and has legalized the issue of such marriage. But her caste tells her that if she follows the law she shall be excommunicated. The latter has proved to be of far greater weight with her than the former, and not even a hundred widow marriages have been celebrated during the last 35 years that the law has been in force. The fact is that the Widow Marriage Act of 1856 was at least thirty years in advance of the community and outside legal circles its existence is known to but few persons, and many a Hindu of the old school would look aghast at being told that the British Government had long ago legalized the remarriage of his widows. Well might he exclaim that Kaliyuga had come ! Widow Marriage Associations have also not been successful in this respect because of the disinclination of the general community to patronize them, and even those who join or sympathize with them have not the courage of their convictions and are thus no better than their less educated brethren. Excommunication to a Hindu is a living death, for no one will have any thing to do with him, no temple will admit him, he is even deserted by his nearest and dearest relatives, his sons and daughters have to remain unmarried unless they are married out of the caste, and if he dies no one will take his body to the burning ground. Unless therefore, caste restrictions were relaxed or caste deprived of its power of excommunication or unless its sympathies were enlisted on the side of progress, no reform in this direction could be sucessfuly carried out. The feeling against the remarriage of widows among the lower classes of Hindus is not at all so

strong as in classes or castes claiming religion or social superiority. For example, among Brahmans, Khshatriyas (Rajputs)
Banias, Kayasths and others whom the pride of wealth or
birth has raised in the social scale, the prohibition is very
strong. But among all the lower tribes of Sudras, Jats, Gujars
&c. widows remarry freely, often the late husband's brother,
or if such a person is not available, any other person, in
spite of the injunctions of the Shastras or the teachings of
the priest. In the North-Western Provinces alone out
of a total population of 3 crores and 80 lakhs only one
crore and 4 lakhs of Hindus or $\frac{1}{4}$th comprising the most
wealthy educated and high-born classes, prohibit their
widows from remarrying. In Punjab the proportion is still
higher viz $\frac{1}{3}$rd and in Mairwara in Ajmere they have a
custom of making a widow choose between a white and
a red cloth, soon after her husband's death. If she chooses
the former she means to remain a widow, if the latter to
remarry, a practice which other people may well take a note of.
Several writers on this subject have thought that it lies within
the power of the British Indian Legislature to remove the
disabilities inflicted by the Hindu ecclesiastical law upon
those who marry widows and that the Government could
forthwith deprive that law of its power of punishing the
parties to a widow marriage. But I am afraid the British
Government could not of itself undertake such legislation
without invoking an amount of opposition which would in
the end defeat the very object of reform. Religion, the
Queen's Proclamation and many other things will be cited
in defence of the present custom even more forcibly than

they have been cited in opposition to the Age of Consent Bill.
It is not so much the injunctions of the Vedas, or Manu or
the Sutras or even the Puranas that bring the weight of their
authority in the matter of excommunications by the members of
a caste, but all these plus custom, and the fight is, as I have already said, more against the latter than against the religious law
of the Hindus. No legislation can force one to eat, drink,
associate or contract marriage relations with another. All
that the severest penal legislation can do is to punish overt
acts of excommunication, and when the people who are
affected by such legislation, avoid committing such acts, no
law would be able to touch them. The alternative attempt
of providing for the celebration of widow-marriages before
a registrar would not also have the effect of removing
the social excommunication that the parties to a widow-marriage
will as heretofore suffer. The safest plan is therefore to leave
the matter to such an alteration in the feelings of the community in this respect as would relax the present disabilities
attending the remarriage of a widow. Such an alteration is
gradually coming on and signs are not wanting of even
the higher castes discussing the question of making excommunications not follow the remarriage of virgin widows.
Such movements are coming to the front in the Banya and
other communities in Delhi, Agra and other places and all
that the reformers can practically do in this respect is to
encourage them with their co-operation. If on the other hand
the community itself so demands it, the Government may
move in the matter and a body like the Social Conference is the
best to represent to the Government the wishes of the

community in this respect. The next question of reform in this matter is whether a Hindu widow who on her remarriage loses her first husband's estate and is thus placed in a worse position than a Hindu widow who while in possession of such an estate is guilty of immorality, should not be allowed to keep such estate. The objection that is urged against this reform is that a Hindu widow succeeds to her husband's estate because of her responsibility for the performance of certain religious acts beneficial to his soul; she succeeds to it because her prayers and sacrifices and the employment of his wealth in religious and charitable objects, would be beneficial to him in another state of existence and because by her remarriage she would be disqualified from performing such acts, she ought to lose the estate she has inherited from him. But whatever may be said in favor of this view, in regard to the estate of a husband who dies intestate, there is nothing to say in its favor regarding one who bequeaths by will his property to his widow, and there is no reason why the law should deprive her of that which her husband well knowing the liberty allowed to his widow in taking a second husband has left for her benefit. On the other hand the present law sets a premium to immorality and discourages a Hindu widow from taking the more honorable course of remarrying. In addition to this when a widow succeeds to her husband's estate subject to the performance of religious ceremonies beneficial to his soul, she should not be allowed to keep it when by her own unchastity she has disqualified herself from performing such ceremonies, and yet contrary to the Hindu law and the Hindu custom, the Privy Council have ruled that subsequent unchastity does not divest her of an estate that has already been vested in her. This ruling is not only opposed to the spirit of the Hindu law which enjoins a life of chastity for a Hindu widow who succeeds to her husband's estate, but to the feelings of nearly the whole of the Hindu community also. In the Courts it is invoked only by the adherents of the profligate or the unchaste widow. It does not assist the cause of female emancipation unless the latter is confounded with unchastity. On the contrary it places a widow who keeps half a dozen paramours in a much better position than one who takes the more honorable course of remarrying. The framers of the Hindu law never contemplated it as the nineteenth century interpretation of their teaching, and while on the one hand it is welll for Hindu society that it is not at all widely known among those who would be likely to profit by it, the Government owe it to the policy they have themselves laid down to abrogate it by legislative enactment.

Another step in the direction of reform and one which would greatly commend itself to the Hindu community would be such an amendment of the law as would make the seducer of a virgin widow punishable in the same way as the seducer of a married woman. To a Hindu the loss of his widowed daughter's or daughter-in-law's honour is as painful as that of his wife's ; and a young, inexperienced Hindu widow goes wrong more often from importunity and the arts of the wicked and the profligate than from choice, and the fact that the offender knows he can escape scot-free makes him the more dangerous to any respectable Hindu family. The condition of other societies supplies no analogy, as there infant or child-marriages are not the rule. On the other hand the laws of native States, like Indore, make such offences legally punishable. Could not the British Legislature do the same on the prosecution of the widow's guardians?

These to my mind are the only lines upon which legislation could proceed in this matter. Much, however, depends upon the community itself in this respect and if they but raise the marriageable age both of boys and girls, they will largely put a stop to the increase of virgin widows and thus deprive the custom of one of its greatest terrors. This is a step which does not clash with custom in the same sense as the introduction of remarriage of widows might, and ought I think to be attempted, at least in their own families, by all reformers. The British Government has done all that it can in respect of legalizing the remarriage of widows. It cannot do more. It now rests with the community itself to bring about such a change in this respect as will make them avail of the law more largely than they have hitherto done.

Other forms of relief may also suggest themselves to those who are or may be inclined the assist the needy or the helpless. In every large town the number of genteel poor widows, who are too proud to beg and who would rather die than lead a life of public beggary, is not small or inconsiderable. In some places private charity relieves their suffering, in others they are exposed so all the miseries of starvation. Having no honourable means of earning a livelihood they live upon either manual labour or incur the risk of going astray. For such in the interests of public morality and charity, something seems necessary to be done. I suggest two remedies. (1) For that large class of its Native servants who get poor pay and often die leaving their families unprovided for, let the Government either have a system of State insurance or a family pension fund, just as it has for its civilians and military officers, and compel every one to subscribe to it. The present institutions which admit Uncovenanted servants as subscribers are very limited in their operation, the Hindu Family Pension Fund being confined to Bengalees and the Uncovenanted Service Fund to Christians only ; while the Post Office only ensures the lives of its own employés. An extension of the latter to all Government servants would save many a Native family from misery after the person who earned for it was dead. (2) The Government may also afford more facilities than they have hitherto done to Hindu widows who are young and capable of learning, in studying medicine, the art of teaching &c. so as to be able to find suitable employment both for their time as well as for earning means of subsistence. On the other hand, one may as well impress upon the orthodox Hindu the fact that there is no greater charity than to relieve the really distressed and that there can be no more deserving object of such charity than a Hindu widow left unprovided for.

(4) OTHER QUESTIONS OF SOCIAL REFORM.

(A) Sea Voyages.

Reform in raising the marriageable age and the removal of caste restrictions on the remarriage of widows, are not the only reforms needed in Hindu society. On the contrary there are many other customs of that society which require to be reformed before it can claim to be the progressive society it was in the past. Ancient Hinduism was a living religion which set its foot upon vice and immorality and did not stand in the way of the progress of its followers. Modern Hinduism is a religion of forms and superstition which, while it does not punish vice and immorality, discourages true progress whether it be by prohibiting voyages to foreign countries or sanctioning extravagance in social and domestic ceremonies or in the way of living. The ancient authorities of the Hindu religion never excommunicated those who undertook voyages to foreign countries. In the Rig Veda, for instance, the shipwreck of Bhujju and his deliverance by the God Aṣhvin are spoken of, and injunctions are given regarding people desiring to acquire wealth praying to the sea. The Sutras of Bhadhayana also speak of people of the north going to sea. Chinese travellers speak of Hindu merchants going to distant countries for purposes of trade. The Hindus are also proved to have had communication with Sumatra, Java and China, and Manu speaks of merchants going on sea voyages and the king levying a toll upon ships. Sea fights are also alluded to. The Mahabharata and the Ramayana speak of Sagara, Krishna and Arjuna having all crossed the ocean. Were it not so India could have not attained that high pitch of perfection which is claimed for it. Foreign travel was never prohibited among Hindus and it is with pain and regret that one notices the present prohibition of sea voyages.

It is thought by some that Budhism with it scrupulous respect for living creatures was the cause of this prohibition and that the Brahmans following the teachings of Buddha, introduced the prohibition into the Hindu Shastras in order to profit by that ignorance which such a prohibition was sure to bring about, and that they prescribed heavy penances in order to deter those who might have otherwise made the attempt. The real reason to my mind, however, lies in the destruction of all political life and with it of all spirit of enterprize among the Hindus. The times have however changed and the number of Hindus of all ranks who go to Europe for purposes of business or study is largely increasing, and the question naturally arises whether caste would be acting wisely in excommunicating these people and depriving itself of the services of some of its best and most enlightened members; or whether the time has not come when in its own interests it should relax its restrictions in welcoming back those who have ventured to cross the Ocean. In my opinion the fault lies both ways—with the caste in being unreasonable enough to excommunicate *all* who undertake foreign travel—,and with the persons who undertake such travel in offending against the rules of their caste by adopting foreign modes of dress, eating food and drinking forbidden liquors, both when they are in foreign countries as well as on their return to India and yet expecting their caste-fellows to welcome them back into their society. On the contrary if both were more reasonable and met each other half way, the difficulty would be more easily solved ; and in this connection I can not do better than repro-

duce here the speech I delivered at the last Social Conference
I said:—

"I should like to say a few words in support of the resolution under discussion. I have had the good fortune of
taking a voyage to England in the company of His Highness
the Maharaja Holkar and am therefore in a position to speak as
to the best means of solving this important question. I believe
it is now-a-days the desire of almost every native of India
to pay a visit to Europe either to complete his education or
to advance his business. But the fear of excommunication
is a great, perhaps the greatest hindrance, in the way of many
who would otherwise have nothing to prevent them from
gratifying their wishes in this respect. Even this morning
some of the leading Hindu bankers of Calcutta, whom I am
glad to see in this Conferenee, told me how desirous they
were of taking a voyage to Europe for purposes of business
and how they were handicapped because of their caste restrictions. This desire coming, as it does, from a section of the
community which has all the influence of a trading community, is a sign of the times in which India is moving and this
Conference could not do better than point out to these and other
people the best and the easiest way of solving the difficulty.
I shall explain this with reference to my own case. To my
mind there appears to be some thing wrong in the way in
which we natives of India conduct ourselves in the matter
of our food, dress and way of living both in England as well
as on our return to India. We adopt foreign modes of dress
and eat forbidden food and on our return cut ourselves off
from our own people, and yet we expect them to meet us

more than half way. With such habits, it is not at all a matter of surprise if we are not received back into our own society. All questions of reform seem now-a-days to resolve themselves into how to carry the more numerous but the comparatively less enlightened portion of the community with the party of progress, and the only possible method to my mind is by earning their sympathy, by living as they do and even making some sacrifices in the shape of conforming to their ways in small matters in order to be able to carry them along with us in questions of more vital importance. The matter was also discussed by the late Public Service Commission in connection with the question of the training of native youths in England both before and after passing the Civil Service Examination, and the Commission said:—
" The witnesses have generally admitted that any inconvenience to which persons who have undertaken a journey to England were subjected on their return to India, was due less to incidents necessarily inherent in the voyage or in residence in England, than to other extraneous circumstances. Such, for instance, as a refusal on their part to subject themselves to the expiatory ceremonies or observances demanded by their fellow-countrymen as a condition to their rehabiliation to caste privileges, or to their having by their own voluntary proceedings premanently placed themselves beyond the pale of caste recognition . In some instances, indeed, the persons referred to had already come under influences in this country which would have separated them from caste sympathies even if they had not gone to England." I believe the conclusions arrived at by the Public Service Commission are corroborated

by the daily experience of native society. For instance in my own case because I steadily adhered to my former habits both in the matter of food as well as in the matter of dress, I was gladly and with open arms welcomed back into my own community, without ever so much as word having been said as to my having lost or not lost my caste, or without my being required to perform any expiatory ceremonies. On the contrary I believe my opportunities for doing good to my own countrymen have in a manner vastly increased by my increased knowledge of English life and English ways of thought, and I am sure the same will be the case with every one else who perfers the good opinion of his own society to any fancied ideas of increased familiarity with foreigners. In England also my Indian dress instead of being a source of disadvantage or discomfort was quite the reverse, and many places which would have not been otherwise open to me, were opened because of that dress. In the matter of food also my habits of vegetarianism were everywhere respected and whether in the palaces of Her Majesty the Queen or the mansions of the rich or the cottages of the poor, wherever I had the honor of being presented or asked to dinner or lunch, my wants were all, as if it were, anticipated. To conclude, I feel that the only possible solution of the question before us lies in the determined resoluion of every Indian who goes to Europe to adhere to his former habits in the way of dress and other things and to use his increased knowledge for the advancement of his countrymen in a manner they may be able to appreciate, in a word, while increasing his knowledge of European sciences, arts, and institutions, to return from Europe with the same habits of simplicity as he had when he left for it. If he does so, his caste will meet him more than half way, very probably it will not even think of excommunicating him at all."

(b) EXTRAVAGANCE IN MARRIAGE AND OTHER CEREMONIES.

Coming now to the question of extravagance in marriage and other ceremonies, it does not require much argument to show that the deep holes which such ceremonies make in the Hindu's pocket require to be filled up before he could be prosperous. Such extravagances are not at all sanctioned by the Hindu religion. On the contrary custom or the practice of the caste is the only justification for those large sums of money that are now thrown away on occasions of births, marriages and other ceremonies. The Hindu who is otherwise very frugal becomes, as if it were, possessed by the demon of extravagance on such occasions, and costly feasts and trumpery shows that are indulged in by him at these ceremonies, reveal how wide apart is his practice from that of his ancestors in the past. His priest and his astrologer who profit by his credulity and whose influence is stronger than that of any Roman Catholic Bishop before the Restoration, instead of discouraging encourage these shows, and thus furnish a strange contrast to their predecessors of old who did not plunder their clients in the way they are now done. Such a state of things requires reform as urgently as early marriages and enforced widowhood. Something of this kind has been attempted by the Rajputs of Rajputanà whose action has been considered to be " the greatest advance made in the century, and might lead to changes which no living man could foresee." Starting with a maximum ⅔ds of an annual income of 1,000 Rupees as the sum allowed to be spent on one marriage, they go on reducing it as they proceed upwards ; for example, in cases of incomes between 1,000 and 10,000 it would be ½, between 10,000 and 20,000, it would be ⅓ and above that ¼. They have also stopped the *tika* or engagement presents as well as fixed the amount of money which is to be given to Bhats &c. They have appointed in every state a Committee consisting of a Sardar, an official and a member of the Charan or the Rao caste, or with such modifications in its constitution as the Durbar may be in favor of, and have required every head of an estate to give a month's previous notice to this Committee in order that the latter may enforce the above regulations. In order to discourage the practice of fathers of girls receiving money from fathers of bridegrooms, they have fixed a limit of Rs 100 which is to be spent in a marriage, and they have provided punishments for those who transgress the rules. The marriageable age for boys has been fixed at 18 and for girls at 14 and no widower who has a son living and has attained the age of 45 is allowed to remarry. They have also prescribed a scale for expenses incurred at funerals, ⅔rd for an income of 1,000, ¼th for an income between 1,000 and 5,000, ⅕th for one between 5,000 and 10,000 and ⅛th for an income above 10,000. The minimum limit is however fixed at 100 for a marriage and 75 for a death.

I have made inquiries as to the practical working of these rules and am told on good authority that though the method of inquiry is not at all satisfactory, nor the rules as regards the marriageable age as well as in regard to expenses observed really in about 60 per cent and openly in about 30 per cent of cases, yet the people are fully conscious of the great advantage of the step. Other communities like the Kayasths and Banias of the North-Western Provinces, have also been attempting to reduce these expenses with more or less success. In connection with this it would be interesting to show that the Moghal Emperor Akbar also ruled that marriages should not take place below the age of puberty, that the consent of the bride and the bridegroom was equally necessary with that of their parents, and that boys were not to marry before their sixteenth and girls before their fourteenth year. The Emperor moreover appointed two disinterested persons, one to ascertain the condition of the men and the other to inform himself of the rank of the women and levied a tax upon all marriages according to the rank of the parties. This tax varied from 10 gold mohurs to one *dam* and the rich as well as the poor all had to pay it without distinction of caste or creed. The Brirish Government could not follow the Moghal Emperor in taxing Hindu marriages. But they may follow him in fixing the marriageable age. The rest is a matter for the community itself, which it is some satisfaction to find is gradually beginning to recognize the extent of the evil.

(c) SHRADDHAS.

The same remarks apply to funeral ceremonies also. In the ancient authorities of the Hindu religion we miss all sanction in favor of the money that is now extorted or the extravagance that is now indulged in on such occasions. The very word *Shraddha* signifies that which is given willingly and from motives of religious faith. The noble object of the ceremony viz. that of constantly reminding the Hindu of his ancestors as well as that of satisfying that innermost craving of the human heart viz. a love of immortality, has been entirely lost sight of in the present doctrine of exchanges of articles of this world for corresponding ones of the next. The Brahmans invited to these ceremonies are not as inculcated by the old Smirti writers like Manu, Vasishta and others, invited in small numbers, nor are they distinguished for learning and virtue, nor are they free from evil marks. The denunciations of Manu that the giver of sacrificial food to a man unacquainted with the Vedas, is sowing seed in barren soil or his indignation at the cat-like propensities of some Brahmins, are moreover not now regarded in practice among the Hindus. A Shraddha of these days is not a ceremonial of love and affection nor are the gifts made at it regulated by the giver's means or made to deserving objects, at the proper time and the proper place. The most respected authorities of the Hindu religion all denounce such gifts and yet they are made and even extorted in the name of religion. Says Krishna in the Bhavadgita " That which is given from a sense of duty without any expectation of return in proper time, at the proper place and to a deserving object is the satvaki (true) gift. On the other hand that which is given without regard to time or place, to a person who does not deserve it, is a (tamasi) gift or one made from ignorance." (Gita—Chap. 17,20 and 22). The Mahabharata also declares gifts to a Brahman that by birth is a Brahman but is destitute of the occupations of his order, to be in vain. " A Brahman " the sage Markandeya said to Yudhishthara

is one " who hath cast off anger and passion, who always speaks
the truth, is cognisant of morals, is catholic in religion, looks
upon all as equal to himself, is of a liberal soul and is vigi-
lantly devoted to the study of the Vedas." * No reform
could therefore be more in harmony with the spirit of the
Hindu religion than to follow the teachings of the great Hindu
writers in the matter of the Shraddha ceremonies, to cut down
all unnecessary expenses, and to see that only those who by
their learning and piety deserve gifts at such ceremonies
receive them.

(d) PILGRIMAGES.

The case with the money thrown away at places of
pilgrimages is also the same. The object of these pilgrimages in the past was very noble. It was to afford the
man of the world as well as the recluse, the opportu-
nity of benefiting from the company of the learned, the
wise and the pious, and only those " whose minds and bodies
were under control, who were free from pride and anger, who
adhered to truth and who regarded all creatures as their own
self" were declared capable of enjoying the fruits of such
pilgrimages. Pilgrimages were "for men without wealth,
without allies and without means. Vedic sacrifices could
only be performed at the expense of money and were
intended for kings and men of wealth. Pilgrimages to
sacred places were on the other hand for those who
could not afford to make sacrifices."† How such a noble
institution has been abused will be seen from the fact that
the money thrown away upon pilgrimages to Gaya, Hardwar,

* Mahabharta Vana Parva Chaps 200 and 206

Benares and other places goes to maintain a class of idlers who spend the hard-earned money of the ryot and the trader in maintaining the liquor shop or the prostitute. Under the garb of religion many of these places prove the ruin of thousands of innocent women. There is no inherent virtue in the places themselves as is conmonly inculcated and it is time that the truth should be impressed upon our people.

(e) General Characteristics of Modern Hindu Society.

A word now as to the general characteristics of modern Hindu society. The sage Markandeya had probably the present times in his mind when he said to the King Yudhiṣthra.

" O Bull of the Bharata race towards the end of the last mentioned period of one thousand years i. e. when the period wanted to complete a cycle is short, men generally become addicted to falsehood in speech. And those things will also be enjoyed by men in such times, the enjoyment of which hath been forbidden in the Scriptures. And the Brahmans speaking disrespectfully of the Vedas, will not practise vows, and their understandings clouded by the science of disputation, they will no longer perform sacrifices and the Homa. And full of avarice and folly, the whole world will have but one kind of food. And *girls of 5 and 6 years of age will bring forth children and boys of 7 or 8 years of age will become fathers.* And without a knowledge of the ordinance, men will perform ceremonies and rites, and, indeed behave as listeth them, when the end of the Yuga comes. And men will be filled with anxiety as regards means of subsistence, trees and gardens will cease to bear fruit. Possessions of men will never be much and the inhabited regions of the earth will be filled with dearth and famine."*

This after allowing for all poetical exaggeration is now more or less the case and instead of the life of an ordinary Hindu being now characterized by all its former simplicity or religiousness, it is now characterized by the too common indulgence in articles of food and drink that are altogether foreign to his religion, his climate and his habits, by his boys and girls becoming fathers and mothers though not at 7 or 8, yet at 12 or 13, by his priests neglecting the study of their religion, by famines and dearths becoming the normal condition of his country, and by his men of education showing more knowledge and more respect for other nations' institutions than their own. Even Englishmen whom our people are so anxious to imitate, condemn the present love of the Indians for things foerign, to the neglect of their own better and more congenial habits whether they appertain to matters of food or dress or way of living. Only the other day, an English gentleman occupying one of the highest positions in India, told me of the way in which certain natives lately returned from England had behaved themselves in his presence, adding that he could not help advising them not to bring the rough manners they had learnt in the west into this land of good manners, the east !

The fact is that, without at all being reactionists, it is time that our people should learn that after all the ancient law-givers and sages of India who regulated the life of the Indian people, were better and more intimately acquainted

* Mahabharata Vana Parva—Chaps. 190.

with the climate of the country as well as the character and habits of its people, than even those who claim to be most learned in western institutions and that while the Indians should go to the west for instruction in its sciences, its arts and its political institutions, they should not neglect the teachings of their own religion or to adhere to what is good in their own institutions.

(f) CONCLUSION.

To conclude. The subject of social reform is to my mind even of greater importance than political reform, for political reform can only be useful when those who seek it are physically, mentally and morally capable of using it to the best advantage. This could not, I am afraid, be said of the Hindu society of the present day. For although indications of progress are most remarkably present in that society now-a-days, yet it has yet to come up to the standard of societies in modern Europe whose institutions it is aiming to follow, or to that of its own institutions in the past. Nations are the masters of their own destiny and no nation has risen in the scale of progress except by honest and unselfish work in the cause of public good. In Hindu society these elements have never been wanting; on the contrary, the charity of that people, their general truthfulness, their rectitude of conduct, their earnest religiousness, have all shown themselves to advantage even under the worst forms of repression. The Hindu nation has never been dead to the teachings of religion; only now-a-days its true and living religion has been made to give place to form and dogma, the teachings of its Valmiki, Vyasa, Vashishta, Manu, Krishna,

Sankaracharya and others, the examples of its heroes of the past, to unmeaning customs and gross superstitions, causing great national deterioration and much injury all round. So that no sincerer prayer could be offered by a well-wisher of that community, than that it may follow its purer and more ancient religion and the teachings of its ancient sages more closely than it is now doing. This it can only do by its own efforts. The Government can only help it to a very limited extent. On the contrary all true reform in the constitution of its society must come from within itself and not from without, and such reform can only come from honest and persistent effort both individual and corporate, and the following quotation from what Vashishta said to Ramchandra may well be laid to heart by all our people " What one desires he attains, if he makes honest effort to attain it. Without effort nothing is attained. The gods have attained to their present position by their own efforts. Persistent effort can even level mountains. What wonder if it can modify the result of one's actions in a previous birth. The actions of one's past life have a tooth and nail struggle with the actions of his present life. Let a man therefore conquer the evil results of the past by good actions in the present. Those who having given up effort, believe in fate are beasts among men, they are the worms of hell. Those who sit silent believing in fate drive away good fortune from their doors. On the other hand those who resolve to conquer fate, do so and attain the objects of all their desires both in this world and the next" *

My visit to England and parts of Europe and my stay there,

* Yog Vasishtha Book II.—Chap. 5.

short though it was, have moreover convinced me even more thoroughly than before, that true progress in a nation can only be achieved by resolute efforts on the part of its members and that before a nation could claim to be truly great, it should advance not only on the lines of political but also of physical, moral, material and above all spiritual activity. My attention was also forcibly directed to the great importance which is attached in European countries to the division of labour in public matters, and nothing struck me more vividly than the fact that almost all the great public men I had met, had made particular subjects of social or political reform their speciality; and I believe that if those of our countrymen who aspire to do public good, were to act on the same lines also, the cause of Indian progress would be more rapid than it has been hitherto. It is not the number of men of education and talent that devote themselves to any one sphere of public activity alone that determines the progress of a country. On the contrary it is the number of its men of activity in all the various spheres of public usefulness that determines it and nothing is more unsatisfactory than to find such an increasingly large number of our men of education and talents treading beaten paths or devoting themselves to the study of questions which have already been taken up by too many of their countrymen. The question of social reform is for instance one of those questions which requires a more urgent solution and many more workers than even the most vexed political question of the day, and any effort made in this direction will produce more substantial and much higher results than can be attained in the field of politics with its distant results. Yet with the exception of a few persons of earnestness, the workers in this field are not only few in number, but the present agitation of these questions has given rise to a class of men, from whose education and knowledge of their countrymen, such an unreasoning defence of the present practices as they are now making, was never expected. Their attitude is, to say the least, dictated by the most suicidal policy imaginable, and nothing could lower them more in the eyes of those from whom they are seeking their well deserved political privileges, than this opposition to measures calculated to prevent that deterioration of the Hindu race which its present customs have admittedly so largely succeeded in bringing about. If the natives of India are standing before England as candidates for civic or political honors, and appeal to the men and women of that country —to the great body of English electors —for the concession of their demands, let them show that they are worthy of the concessions they pray for by carrying out the necessary social reforms in their own society. The struggle is not now confined to India. It has gone to England. The eyes of the men and women of England are upon the condition of the women of India and the home life of the Hindus, and if they but bring their influence to bear upon the men of England in making the Government ameliorate the condition of Indian women by doing for them what Indian reformers have failed to do, no Government will be able to resist them nor any demonstrations held in India divert them from their object. Such a contingency will, I hope, never come to pass, but, if it does, we ourselves shall be to blame. I conclude with the following prayer from the Upanishads—"Lead us from the unreal to the real. May we conduct ourselves like men o good judgment and devoted to duty. May we proclaim th right ; may we proclaim the true."

BY THE SAME AUTHOR:

In the press and will be shortly ready

FIRST IMPRESSIONS OF AN EDUCATED HINDU OF ENGLAND AND PARTS OF EUROPE.

REPRINTED FROM THE INDIAN SPECTATOR

CONTENTS:—The Voyage.—Aden.—The Suez Canal.—Port Said.—La Belle France.—Paris.—To England, the Home of my Masters.—Parliament.—Public Men.—Politics.—Clubs and Club Politicians.—English Eloquence.—Parliamentary Procedure.—Non Political Associations—At Court.—The Queen —Some Jubilee Reminiscences.—Queen's Palaces.-Indians at Court.—Literary Activity. — Newspapers.—Public Opinion.—Law and Lawyers.—Judges—Criminals.—Witnesses.—The Justice of the Peace and the Police. English Universities.— Educational Facilities for Indian Education.—Mass Education.—Amusements.—Music.—Dancing.—Theatres.—Boat Races.—London Streets.—Religion.—Churches and Churchmen.—The Poor and the Rough in the Streets —Parks—Out in the Suburbs.—Crystal Palace.— Hampton Court.— Kew.—Woolwich.—Enfield.—Leamington.—Warwick.— Manchester.—Liverpool. — Birmingham. — Scotland. — Edinburgh.— Glasgow. — The Continent.—Switzerland. — Italy.—Milan. — Rome.——Naples.—Alexandria.—Egypt.—Conclusion.

The writer, as might be expected, has all throughout compared Indian matters with what he came across in Europe, and his Impressions have not only been largely quoted in Indian papers, but as the following editorial note by the *Indian Spectator* will show, been appreciated in England and France.

" This week we conclude a very interesting series started in our columns about six months ago, being " First Impressions of an educated Hindu, of England and of Parts of Europe." The writer is a well-known Indian graduate, a reformer engaged in the social as well as the political sphere, wherein he has done excellent service. As an officer of Government he is held in esteem by some of our best administrators, and his work has always evinced a quick eye and a steady hand. The Impressions, which he has so cleverly jotted down in these columns, have been appreciated in India as also in England and France."

LEGAL MAXIMS

IN URDU

ILLUSTRATED AND EXPLAINED WITH SPECIAL REFERENCE TO THE LAWS IN FORCE IN BRITISH INDIA, THE HINDU AND THE MAHOMEDAN LAWS,

AND

PRECEDENTS OF THE HIGH COURTS AND THE PRIVY COUNCIL.

" An admirable and useful compendium of *Legal Maxims* in Urdu. Those engaged in legal studies will find this book valuable and important, as explaining the governing rules of jurisprudence and the mode in which they are applied in legislation and judicial decision. The compiler is to be congratulated on the mode in which he has accomplished his task. (*Pioneer.*)

The work is a monument of research, labour, patience and considerable legal and literary acquirements. The book is quite unique, and has no rival, either in English or in Hindustani, Professor Broom's or any other book which is considered an authority on the subject of legal maxims having no special reference to the laws of India. The explanations are long and lucid, and free from such technicalities as may not be easily understood by laymen; and though the author as a Hindoo modestly gives up all claim to elegance of diction, the language of his book has the valuable recommendation of perspicacity and conciseness. We congratulate Lala Baijnath on the excellent book that he has just brought out, and we hope he will find time to continue his legal labours for the benefit of his countrymen. *Indian Chronicle.*

It is altogether a valuable work of reference, and as such ought to find a place in the library of every native lawyer. *The Statesman.*

The compiler is to be complimented on the considerable care and trouble he has taken in accomplishing his task. *Indian Jurist.*

It seeks to place within the reach of native lawyers a knowledge of the principles of law in a handy and popular form and is a valuable addition to vernacular literature, and taken as a whole the arrangement seems to be both clear and comprehensive. The book is arranged in the best manner possible to facilitate reference. We would not be worng in saying that it ought to find a place in the library of every Native lawyer. *Indian Spectator.*

This is a really well written book, and it deserves the attention of the bench and the bar as well of those engaged in legal studies. We hope that both as an encouragement to Native authors and Translators as well as in recognition of the learned author's ability, industry and enterprise, the public will also not fail to largely patronize it. *(Oudh Akhabar)*

Price Rs. 6 post free V. P. P. extra.

Hints on the trial of Civil Suits in Urdu	8 annas.
Principles of Hindusim explained in Urdu with quotations from the Shasters.	4 annas.

Postage extra.

Social Reform in the N. W.-P.

Mr. Baijnath is one of the most enlightened, earnest and temperate of Hindu reformers, and his observations on the evils of Infant-marriage, and caste and enforced widowhood require the most careful attention of his countrymen. As we said at the time, the resolution of the Government on the subject ought by no means to be taken to mean that remedial legislation is finally refused. On the contrary the reformers should redouble their efforts to impress the people with the evils of the existing system and to demonstrate that its abolition is in no way opposed to the precepts of their religious lawgivers in their original purity.

It is with the object of enforcing this view of the matter that Mr. Baijnath has written his pamphlet. All he wants is that when the Local Legislature is established in these provinces, the leaders of the community may be able to show that their views are sufficiently representative to justify legislative action. If this end is to be attained, it must certainly be by such efforts as Mr. Baijnath is making. (*Pioneer.*)

Apply

. to the author, or to Manager, "Voice of India", 24 Hornby Road, Bombay.

9781535811088